A MISCELLANY OF DISPUTES

The arbitration scene from Menander's *The Arbitrants*, after a mosaic found in 'Menander's House' in Mytilene, on the island of Lesbos, dating from c. AD 350.

A MISCELLANY OF DISPUTES

Derek Roebuck

HOLO BOOKS

THE ARBITRATION PRESS
OXFORD

Published by The Arbitration Press
A division of HOLO Books
Clarendon House
52 Cornmarket Oxford OX1 3HJ

Copyright © 2000 Derek Roebuck

The right of Derek Roebuck to be identified
as the author of this work has been asserted
by him in accordance with the Copyright,
Designs and Patents Act 1988

British Library Cataloguing in Publication Data
A catalogue record for this book is available
from the British Library

ISBN 0-9537730-0-0

Designed, typeset and produced for
HOLO Books: The Arbitration Press by
Chase Production Services,
Chadlington, OX7 3LN
Printed in the European Union

CONTENTS

Foreword by Neil Kaplan, QC		7
Preface		10
1	WITHOUT THE LAW	14
2	A FAMILY AFFAIR	30
3	GODS, GODDESSES AND HEROES	41
4	WOMEN AND ARBITRATION	49
5	THE SORROWS AND REWARDS OF THE ARBITRATOR	63
6	UNHAPPY PARTIES	73
7	LANGUAGE TRAPS	89
8	UMPIRES	96
9	ARBITRATION ON THE STAGE	102
Index		120
About the Author		126

To the President, Fellows, Members and Associates
of the Chartered Institute of Arbitrators

FOREWORD

It is a pleasure to be able to contribute a Foreword to Derek Roebuck's latest addition to legal history and scholarship.

Ever since I was a student I have been fascinated by the two *Miscellanies-at-Law* written by Sir Robert Megarry. I was therefore delighted when Derek Roebuck found enough material to warrant this *Miscellany of Disputes.*

When I first suggested to him that he might like to write a brief history of arbitration as an introduction to a book that others and I were writing on Hong Kong arbitration law, little did I know what interest the subject would provoke in his ever-enquiring mind. Several years later, and well into the subject, he has got as far as the Greeks. He has unearthed much new material and in due course I am sure he will give us the *locus classicus.*

However, for the moment we have to be grateful for the fact that his research for materials on arbitration has unearthed much interesting and amusing material which he has brought together in this first anthology of stories about disputes resolved without access to the traditional courts. As such, I am sure it will be of interest to all concerned with arbitration and a useful tool for speechmakers, given the unfortunate paucity of usable material on arbitration.

The practice of arbitration can have its lighter

moments. Evidence through interpreters is often a case in point. In one case where a witness was being affirmed, the affirmation was translated as: 'I solemnly declare and affirm that I will tell nothing of the truth.' Cultural and linguistic differences also throw up amusing results. In one case an English barrister was cross-examining a Chinese witness through an interpreter. The case concerned defective jeans. Counsel asked the witness to say what he did when the jeans were delivered. 'I rang the factory.' 'What did they say?' The witness said that he could not follow the question. The exasperated barrister insisted: 'You told us that you telephoned the factory. Now please tell us *precisely* what they said when they answered the telephone.' With a smile of relief, tinged with comprehension, the witness replied: 'Hello!'

It is not only through the use of foreign languages that amusing results occur. In one case the arbitrator was using *Livenote*, a system whereby a legal stenographer takes the evidence down on a machine, which instantaneously transforms it into a transcript on the computer screens which all the participants have in front of them. An American attorney was cross-examining an American witness: 'And what were you doing while Mr X was *schlepping* this agreement around town?' Neither witness nor counsel could understand the mirth that ensued because they were too involved to be watching their screens, which were showing: 'And what were you doing while Mr X was sleeping around town?'

I must resist the temptation to write another chapter for this *Miscellany*. There is enough there already to keep the reader occupied and, who knows, we may get a second *Miscellany* as the author unearths more fascinating material which shows that the problems which we grapple with today have all been grappled with before. In this field, as in so many others, it can truly be said that there is nothing new under the sun.

Derek Roebuck is to be congratulated for having found time to put this *Miscellany* together as a by-product of his main *History of Arbitration*, the publication of which we look forward to with anticipation.

Neil Kaplan QC
President of the Chartered Institute of Arbitrators

PREFACE

An anonymous letter to *The Times* of 11 August 1892 declared:

> The mercantile public is not fond of law, if law can be avoided. They prefer even the hazardous and mysterious chances of arbitration in which some arbitrator who knows as much of the law as he does of theology, by the application of a rough and ready moral consciousness, or upon the affable principle of dividing the victory equally between both sides, decides intricate questions of law and fact with equal ease.

It has always been thought that the letter was written by Lord Justice Bowen. It reveals a judicial impatience with arbitration that may be understandable and even justifiable from time to time.

Lord Campbell, a Lord Chancellor whose own sense of humour was unpleasantly mordant, quotes the humourist John Anstey with approval.[1] He portrays the lawyer as the devotee of strife, praying that no dispute should be brought to an amicable settlement:

> Come then, thou Goddess of Contention,
> Genius of Craft and Circumvention,
> You, who in parchment robes array'd

---

1 John Lord Campbell *The Lives of the Chief Justices of England from the Norman Conquest to the Death of Lord Tenterden* London John Murray 2nd edn 3 vols 1858 III p271.

> And tape-tied vest of vellum made,
> With ink-stained lips, and eyeballs blear'd,
> And thumbs with wax and rosin smear'd,
> The baleful bitter drafts prepare
> Of Poverty, Revenge, and Care,
> And every tender tie remove
> Of Amity and Social Love ...[2]

And the lawyer curses those who, by mediation, arbitration or otherwise, try to bring about the peaceful resolution of disputes:

> Then woe to him who would devise
> Pacific schemes of compromise;
> Perish the man who dares control
> That generous ardour of the soul,
> That noble, that ingenuous heat
> Which prompts the truly brave and great,
> To seek an adversary's ruin,
> Though purchas'd by his own undoing.
> May the fat weed of Lethe shed
> Its dullness o'er his recreant head,
> Whoe'er has wilfully suppress'd
> That passion in his client's breast!
> May he, in self-condemning mood,
> For lack of more substantial food,
> *Eat his own soul*!

Such heated animosity hides the usual reality, that law and arbitration have lived together from time imme-

---

[2] John Anstey *The Pleader's Guide, a Didactic Poem in Two Books; Containing the Conduct of a Suit at Law, with the Arguments of Counsellor Bother'um and Counsellor Bore'um in an Action between John-a-Gull and John-a-Gudgeon for Assault and Battery at a Late Contested Election. By the late John Surrebutter Esq., Special Pleader and Barrister-at-Law* London 1796, quoted in David Murray *Lawyers' Merriments* Glasgow 1912 [*Murray*] pp71–74.

morial; for the most part in harmony. Few would now deny, or ever have, that most disputes can be resolved without litigation, and even without the law. Sometimes, it would seem, with greater justice.

You who read this little book may be surveyors, who regularly wrestle with disputes between those reasonable and placatory practitioners who make the construction industry such a haven of tranquillity; or merchants, pinching and sniffing their way through the vintage remains of what were once the raw materials of food; or the demigods of the profession, the international arbitrators, who hear great advocates crossing language barriers with the same apparent ease with which they invade foreign jurisdictions.

More likely, you will not be the sort of person who could ever figure in this book, or at least not as the arbitrator in the first story. For you it will be justified only if it tells a good tale. I have gone to the original sources wherever I could and made my own translations but have had no compunction in embellishing an anecdote or telling it in my own way.

Sources in Latin and Greek are cited from Loeb Classical Library editions, published by Heinemann, London, and now by Harvard University Press, Cambridge, Massachusetts.

Footnotes are pretentious in a work like this, but never mind.[3] I have complained so much about the

---

[3] And, without them, you could trace most of the authorities anyway in my 'Sources for the History of Arbitration' (1998) 14:3 *Arbitration International* 237–343.

lack of an index in other books that I felt obliged to append one even to this.

I am especially grateful to Neil Kaplan for writing the Foreword and, even more, for the priceless gift he mentions there, of having put together in my mind for the first time the words 'arbitration' and 'history'. It is gratifying to be able to dedicate this little book to those in the Chartered Institute of Arbitrators, who do so much to foster the amicable resolution of disputes, in which good humour plays its part.

Derek Roebuck
Oxford
November 1999

1
WITHOUT THE LAW

The Simple-Minded Arbitrator

A poor man, with only a few pennies in his pocket and a loaf of bread, took advantage of the delicious smells pouring from a café window. Alternating mouthfuls of bread with sniffs of relish, he enjoyed a satisfying meal.

Out came the cook:

'What are you up to?'
'Drinking in the smell of your delightful cooking.'
'Well, pay for it then!'

The poor man was astonished. He had only a handful of coins and he had intended no purchase. The cook threatened him with the law and, to avoid it, the poor man agreed to the ad hoc arbitration of the next person who passed by. It happened to be a man reputed to be simple-minded. He listened carefully to the evidence. The facts were not in dispute. He gave his award on the spot.

To the cook: 'Fetch me two tin basins!'
To the poor man: 'Hand me your pennies!'

The simpleton put the coins in one basin and covered it with the other. Then he shook them at the cook.

'You hear that? The sound of his money is due payment for the smell of your food.'

The Parties' Choice

William West, who wrote that story,[1] would perhaps have agreed with the Roman jurist Pomponius[2] in disqualifying 'a person who, by nature or accident, has not discretion'; and Comyn's *Digest*[3] doubted whether 'persons of non sane memory' could be appointed. The Common Law at first hesitated, wanting it both ways. Matthew Bacon, in one of the first textbooks on arbitration law in English, prevaricated:[4]

> It is often said, and almost established as a Rule, that neither natural nor legal Disabilities do hinder anyone from being an Arbitrator; for if they are incompetent Judges, the Fault is in those who choose them; but they must, notwithstanding this, have some common Sense, as well as common Honesty.

But a few years later he got it right in his *New Abridgment*:[5]

1 In his *Symboleography Part I: which may be termed the Art or Description of Instruments, Contracts and Presidents, augmented. Part II Four Treatises: 1. Fines and Concordes; 2. Common Recoveries; 3. Offences and Indictments; 4. Compromises and Arbitrements* London Tothill Pt I 1590; Pt II 1594. This story comes from Pt II section 24.
2 Of the second century AD, followed in Justinian's *Corpus Juris*, in the great compendium of legal opinions called the *Digest* at 8, 4.
3 *A Digest of the Laws of England by ... Sir John Comyns* 4th edn by Samuel Rose 6 vols London Strahan 1800 I p519.
4 *The Compleat Arbitrator or the Law of Awards and Arbitraments by a Gentleman of the Middle Temple* London John Worrall 1731 p9.
5 *New Abridgment of the Law* 5 vols London various publishers 1736–1766 I, *arbitrament*.

The Arbitrators are persons indifferently chosen to determine the matters in controversy according to their own mind whether they be matters of law or fact. Infants, persons excommunicate, outlawed &c may be arbitrators, for every person must use his own discretion in the choice of his judges and being at liberty to chuse whom he likes best cannot afterwards object the want of honesty or understanding to them or that they have not done him justice.

There are no decided cases on this point. It would seem unlikely that many parties have intentionally appointed someone they knew to lack mental capacity, though quite likely that some have suspected they have done so when it was too late.

The Scholar Arbitrator

It is almost as unpredictable to submit your dispute to a scholar as to a simpleton.[6] Two neighbouring farmers were sitting and chatting. Wong told Chang his dreams: 'If only I had a hundred acres of paddy field I'd be happy.' Chang replied: 'If you had a hundred acres of paddy, I'd raise ten thousand ducks and they'd fly over and eat it all up.' 'You wouldn't,

---

6 I found this story in Lu Yunzhong *100 Chinese Jokes through the Ages* (in Chinese and English) printed in Hong Kong 1994, quoting Shi Chengjin *Xiao de Hao or It's Good to Laugh* 163 Stories of the Qing Dynasty.

you know, because that would be illegal.' 'Not a bit of it – I'd be perfectly within my rights.'

And so the row flared up and they went in search of the local official to arbitrate for them. Unfamiliar with such matters, they mistook a stately school house for the town hall. Entering with trepidation, they met a scholarly man in the courtyard and put their dispute to him, in detail and with much elaboration. At last he was able to announce: 'You, Mr Wong, if you ever have the luck to come into the money, may go and buy your hundred acres. And you, Mr Chang, may buy and raise your ducks. And then, if I ever have the good fortune to pass my examinations and become an official, I'll deliver my award.'

The Practical Magistrate

Just because a man is a magistrate does not mean that he knows any law. Nor, indeed, that he needs to know any. Three centuries before William West's time, an anonymous author wrote a manual, *The Institucion of a Gentleman*,[7] in which he suggested that a gentleman living in the country could help the community by becoming a justice of the peace: 'as a stay for simple men and help of their causes by way of arbitration'.

---

7 Anon Bodleian Library Douce G 59, London 1555, see JR Lander *English Justices of the Peace 1461–1509* Gloucester Alan Sutton 1989 pp84–6, 169–70.

West wrote of such a magistrate,[8] faced with an unreasonable complaint.

A man found a purse and at once sought the owner and gave it back to him. The owner, suspicious, counted the coins inside: 'There are only twenty here. There were twenty-one when I lost it.' The owner dragged the finder before the amateur magistrate, who was famous for knowing no law. He listened carefully to the evidence of both sides and gave his award:

> 'You say the purse you lost had twenty-one coins in it. This one had only twenty. Therefore this purse cannot be yours. The applicable law is: finders keepers! Now you, go and have another look for *your* purse, the one with the twenty-one coins in it. We'll all come and help you, if you like.'

Hear Both Sides

The first sighting of the rule of natural law, that became the Roman *audi alteram partem!* appears in *The Precepts of Chiron* attributed to Hesiod by Plutarch:[9] 'Never make a judgment before you have heard the stories of both sides.' The Athenians were fond of proclaiming themselves the guardians of all that was best in Greek culture and contrasting their way of life with that of Sparta. But they had a romantic respect for some of the attributes of their traditional enemies.

---

8 West calls him a justice of a municipal corporation in contrast to a justice of the peace in the country.
9 Loeb *Plutarch: Moralia* XIII p1034.

The Spartan Way

No doubt it is originally an Athenian story which Plutarch tells of two men who wanted to avoid the rigours of a trial but made the mistake of appointing an arbitrator with a Laconic sense of humour. They submitted their dispute to the Spartan king, Archidamus II (469–427 BC). He took them to the temple of Athene of the Brazen House and made them swear to abide by his award, whatever it was. 'Right', he said, 'You both stay here till you have made up your quarrel.'[10]

The One-Eyed Assessor

Even if the arbitration, or expert assessment, comes on appeal before a court, the judges may dispose of it in a way which ignores the law.[11]

A farmer put a price of £20 on his horse. A neighbour was willing to buy but thought the price

---

10 Loeb *Plutarch: Moralia* III p218.
11 Loeb *Babrius and Phaedrus* pp568–9. The most complete and accessible collection of Aesop's fables is the new translation in Penguin Classics: Olivia and Robert Temple *The Complete Fables: Aesop* Harmondsworth Penguin 1998 [*Temple*]. But this fable is not included, being, like most of the good arbitration fables, from long after the time of Aesop, who lived in the early sixth century BC.

too high. They agreed to abide by the assessment of its value by the first person they met when they got to town. That person happened to be a man with one eye. He fixed the price at £10. The prospective buyer accepted the assessment, the seller refused. The appeal went to three judges. The buyer relied on the agreement the parties had made to submit to the expert. The seller's defence was that, as the assessor had only one eye, he could see only half the horse and valued it accordingly. The judges declared the whole matter a great joke and sent the farmer off with his horse unsold.

The Chinese Way: A Ming Answer

Chinese literature is full of traditional stories of methods of resolving disputes without the benefit of the law. That officials were never true judges is shown by their scant observance of the law, if they knew it and if there was any for them to know. The result could be crude. In the Ming Dynasty (AD 1368–1644) a dispute over land was disposed of when the official, like the three appeal judges in the last story, became impatient. He declared that the land was not worth the trouble it was causing and should be forfeited to the emperor.[12]

---

12 Lian Ming Gong An III: *Jin Hou Pan Zheng Shan An*.

A Legalist?

From time to time the followers of Confucius have had to compete with the philosophers of other schools, the Legalists and the Taoists. A Legalist official – who scarcely seems to have earned that adjective – laid down a law that all disputes within his jurisdiction should be settled by an archery contest, to the exclusion of any consideration of law or merits. That would discourage claims and encourage proper preparation for war.[13]

Confucius and Mao Tse-tung

Even today, there are deep-seated influences which militate against litigation and the rule of law. One is that traditionally in China there has never been a separation of civil from criminal law or of the judiciary from administration. Another is the assumption that all dealings must be fair, with benefit to both sides; otherwise the state wants nothing to do with them. It was as obnoxious to Mao as to Confucius that one side should take advantage of an unequal bargain; and to both of those influential ideologues expediency and the maintenance of harmony were much more

---

13 *Hanfeizi: Neichushuoshang.*

important than truth or justice, never mind legal principles.

Most important is the strength of traditional relations, strongest within the family, sometimes still extended to the clan, and next within the geographical community. Awards of arbitrators and judgments of courts may still, in practice, have to pass tests of fairness and expediency before they are enforced by local officials or judges, whatever the law may say or the highest authorities enjoin. And disputes between individuals are easily characterised as between groups, and people from the same province are often regarded as one group.

The Community Car

This is a typical recent example.[14] During the trial of an economic dispute between a business entity in Shangrao (a county in Jiangxi province) and one in Pucheng (a county in Fujian province), the Pucheng People's Court lawfully took possession of a vehicle belonging to the Shangrao party. In retaliation, people from Jiangxi lured a driver from Pucheng to Shangrao and grabbed his car, saying: 'The Pucheng People's Court has detained our car, so we have detained one

---

14 W Yuen (Wong Kwok-Yuen) and Derek Roebuck 'The Influence of Traditional Morality on the Enforcement of Foreign Arbitral Awards in China' (1996) 2 *Yearbook Law and Legal Practice in East Asia* Kluwer 1996 pp29–53 at 42–3, citing 'A Letter from a Reader' (1991) *China Lawyer* p45.

from Pucheng.' The officials in Shangrao refused to intervene. In rural areas, people still perceive local officials as 'parent officers' and go to them rather than the courts with their disputes, relying on them not for dispassionate assessment but protection of their interests. If the officials in Shangrao had ordered the car to be returned to the Pucheng driver, they would have been blamed for the loss to the local economy.

The Confucian Official

The tales which endure are mostly of the cleverness of Confucian officials called on to deal with disputes on the facts. Confucianism demanded high standards of morality: do not do to others what you would not like them to do to you. But the greatest respect was paid to those who knew how to manipulate the system. To be promoted to high public office, where one might be called on to arbitrate the disputes of others, one needed not only ability but a virtuous reputation.

An elder brother had won high office and wanted to get similar promotions for his two younger brothers. He was the executor of their father's estate and gave himself much more than the share to which he was entitled. The brothers accepted this unfairness meekly and won great renown for their morality and filial piety. When news of their virtue came to the ears of the high officals, they were given public office. At once the elder brother redistributed his own share of the estate to his brothers, giving them far more than they would have been entitled to. His fame lives for ever in the annals.15

But one can go too far. The man who won a reputation for filial piety by apparently living for twenty years in his parents' tomb was punished when it was found he had fathered five sons in that time.16

Shame the Mediator

For Confucians, the aim was to protect the equilibrium by the avoidance of disputes. They believed it was achievable and there were myths of how it had been achieved. One described how, during the Zhou dynasty (1122–256 BC), when Zhou Wen Wang governed in Xi Zhou, there were no disputes, and not a single crime for forty years. Zhou was such an able mediator that people from outside the kingdom flocked to Xi Zhou to seek his assistance. But, so the story goes, once they got there and saw how tranquil it was, they were so ashamed that they resolved their differences themselves.17

---

15 My Chinese friends love to pretend bewilderment when I ask for more precise dating, whether of a pot or a story. It should be enough for me to know that this is a story from the Qing Dynasty. I suspect it comes from the early part of the period AD 1644–1911. I am indebted for most of my Chinese sources to my former colleague and student Wong Kwok-Yuen, who gave me this one from *Hou Han Shu: Xu Jing Zhuan*.
16 *Chen Fan Zhuan*.
17 *Shi Ji: Zhou Ben Ji*.

The Good and Bad Sons

Shame was a valuable aid in dissipating conflict. A man was brought before the official for not looking after his mother. The official decided to punish him with a beating but discussed the matter first with his own mother. She said: 'He has not been well brought up. You can't punish him for that. Why don't you try this instead? Ask his mother to come to stay with me and take him to stay with you. He will be able to see how a good son treats his mother.' After a few days the neglectful son fell on his face before the official and swore to treat his mother as he now knew he should, 'kowtowing until there was blood on his face'.[18]

Unfortunately, the source does not say what the ill-treated unsuccessful mother learned from her visit to the model mother.

Bees and Drones

An arbitrator may well do better to stick to expert knowledge of the construction business and avoid the legal niceties. Phaedrus tells the story of the dispute between the bees and the drones.[19]

---

18 *Wei Shu: Lie Nu: Fang Ai Qin Qi Cui Shi Zhuan*.
19 Loeb *Babrius and Phaedrus* Babrius fable 13.

The bees had a dispute with the drones about who owned the honeycombs. They agreed that the wasp should arbitrate it, being well acquainted with both sides and with the technical engineering side of hive construction. The wasp agreed but expressed concern about her ability to apply the highly technical law of property. 'You all look the same, in shape and colour', she said. 'I don't want to make any mistake, so what I suggest is this practical test. Both sides must fill these wax cells with their distinctive product and then we'll see which most resembles the disputed honeycombs in taste and appearance.'

The bees happily accepted the test; not surprisingly the drones rejected it. But both sides had sworn to accept the wasp's award. She pronounced it: 'It is clear who made the honeycombs. The bees did. The drones could not have done so in a million years. Therefore I declare the bees to be the legal owners of the honeycombs.'

Then Phaedrus makes a somewhat cryptic point: 'I would have passed over this fable in silence if the drones had not broken faith in their agreement.' What he meant was that, in looking through the manuscript of Aesop's fables, to choose which he should turn into Latin verse, he might not have bothered with this one if it had not been so pertinent to his own situation. Other writers were imitating him without acknowledgement. He leaves us in little doubt who the drones were.

The Over-Confident Roebuck

There is nothing worse than an arbitrator too bored with the job to take it seriously; and it never does to assume that you have got the award you want until it is enforced.[20]

A roebuck and a hedgehog were partners in a cornfield. They took it in turns to guard it from other beasts. When it was the roebuck's turn, instead of keeping intruders out, it joined them in stealing much of the growing crop. The hedgehog took over and guarded the field well, allowing no trespassers in. When it came time to divide up the crop, the roebuck wanted half. 'Not likely!' said the hedgehog.

They agreed to submit their dispute to a boar. The boar managed with difficulty to hear out the whole story but he cared little for the niceties of law or fact. He was keen to get rid of responsibility as quickly and easily as he could. His award was that not only the whole crop but ownership of the field as well should go to whichever of the parties should come first in a cross-country race, to be held the next day.

The hedgehog was dismayed and went home in despair. 'Don't worry', said his clever wife, 'We'll win, you just see. What we'll do is this. Think about it – nobody can tell us apart. So, you start off with the stag. Soon everyone will leave you behind and not

---

20 Loeb *Babrius and Phaedrus* p566.

notice you've dropped out. But I'll be waiting near to the finish and will pop up on the line as they all arrive.' That is how it turned out. Mrs Hedgehog crossed the line just as the roebuck raced to the finish.

2

A FAMILY AFFAIR

Not all brothers are as concerned with one another's welfare as the Confucian officials in the last chapter. Nor are all mothers so high-minded. Family disputes can test any system.

The Education of the Selfish Brothers

Two brothers were fighting over the inheritance of their father's land. The father had left a letter directing that the land should go to his grandchild, the eldest son of the elder son. But he had also left a will which contradicted the letter, giving the same land to his younger son. The matter had been brought before the elders of the clan but the brothers refused to accept their jurisdiction, bringing great shame to all.

At last the matter came before the local official. The facts were not in dispute but he could find no law on the point to help him to a decision. No doubt he could just have divided the land in half. But that would not have dealt with the problem as he saw it, the brothers' – and the community's – lack of moral development.

He decided that the brothers should be taught some lessons. First, respect for their father's memory. So he announced that the dispute was all the father's fault and he should be punished. The official threatened to open his coffin and expose his body. The brothers pleaded with him and he agreed to adjourn and postpone that step for the present.

When the brothers were brought back before him, he declared that the appropriate method of continuing would be to test the brothers by torture. They would both be tortured and the first to yield would lose the land. Perhaps they would each be kind enough to offer to the torturer the leg which they thought would feel less pain. They began to get the message. Again they pleaded with the official. Again he agreed to postpone that part of the trial and adjourned, keeping them in custody.

When the hearing restarted, he ordered that the brothers, now much more subdued, should be chained together. At first they turned their backs in silent hatred. But after a few days they sighed and glanced at one another. Eventually they whispered to each other their remorse. They agreed to make up their quarrel and asked to be brought back before the official.

When the hearing resumed, he told them they were in such trouble because their father had had two sons. Obviously, that was not the sort of problem their family could cope with. He intended to ensure it could not happen in the next generation. So, he ordered each of them to send for adoption all but one of their sons. Horrified, both brothers asked to be allowed to give the disputed land to a temple. The hearing was adjourned.

Then the official questioned all the members of the family to make sure they all felt confident that the brothers had had a genuine change of heart. Only when he was satisfied that they and the whole community, as well as the brothers, had learned their lesson, did the official call them all together to hear his award, which vested the land in the brothers in common.[1]

---

1 *Lan Ding Yuan Lu Zhou Gong An Ou Ji Shang: Xiong Di Song Tian*. A much fuller version, with a chapter devoted to the roles of the brothers' wives, is in Richard Van Over (ed.) *Smearing the Ghost's Face with Ink: a Chinese Anthology* London Picador 1982 pp152–9.

Apollo and his New Half-Brother

Even divine brothers can have disputes.[2] No sooner was Hermes born than he was up to mischief. First he killed a tortoise and used its shell to invent the seven-stringed lyre. Then he stole his half-brother Apollo's cattle, driving them backwards to cover their tracks. When Apollo searched him out, he was already snuggled up again in his cradle, pleading his newborn innocence. Apollo carted him off to their father Zeus (Jupiter), king of the gods, to sort out their dispute.

Zeus sarcastically asks Apollo wherever he could have found such a big, bonny babe, 'a new born baby built like a policeman. This must be a *very* weighty matter that comes before the gods' official assembly!' Apollo doesn't think it funny. He begins his case:

> 'Father, you'll soon find out that this is no laughing-matter. I know you're always saying it's me who's fond of loot. Let me tell you, I've had to travel miles, all the way to the hills of Cyllene to track down this child, the thieving little rustler. I've never seen such a precocious cheat in all the world, god or man. He stole the cattle out of my field and drove them off in the evening along the beach, all the way to Pylos. He left tracks all right – but you'd never believe it, the clever little devil – the

---

2 In the Homeric Hymn *To Hermes*, probably composed in the seventh century BC in Loeb *Hesiod* pp362–405.

dark dust showed the cattle's tracks leading *backwards*, back to my field of asphodel. There were no signs of him walking in the sand, the crafty fellow, he couldn't have been walking, neither on his feet nor his hands. However he did it, I think he must have found some means of covering his tracks by wearing slender oak twigs on his feet.'

Zeus asks Hermes what he has to say for himself. He is already the complete lawyer:

'I shall put my case simply and truthfully. These are the several grounds of my defence. First, Apollo can produce no witnesses. Secondly, I have never confessed anything but, if I had, my confession is inadmissible. He tried to get it out of me by threats of violence. Thirdly, I am below the age of legal responsibility for any criminal offence. I was only born yesterday. Fourthly, rustlers are great big chaps and I'm only little. Fifthly, I wouldn't ever tell a lie to my father. Sixthly, I will swear a great oath to prove I'm innocent.[3] And lastly, you should be on my side anyway because I'm younger than him.'

Hermes is still clad only in his nappy. Zeus roars with laughter at his tricks. He puts his arm round both of

---

3 Hermes was precociously clever but clearly he had not yet learned the sanctions on gods who swear a false oath on the waters of the Styx. In the *Theogony* 782–804 Hesiod describes the process and punishment. Iris is sent to get the water in a golden jug. The oath-taker pours it out and swears on it. If forsworn, the god falls into a coma for one year and then is barred from the gods' assembly for a further nine. Apollo's first friendly gesture then, obvious to all but Hermes, is to save him from the risk of this punishment.

them and tells them to make up their quarrel. But he tells Hermes he'd better take Apollo to where he has hidden the cattle.

Hermes shows Apollo where the cattle are but two have already been eaten. Apollo is furious but Hermes sings and plays on the lyre. Apollo is charmed and says that the song is worth fifty cows: 'I don't think we'll have much difficulty in coming to a settlement. By this staff I declare, just as if we were in the assembly, that this is my exact suggestion for a settlement. I'll give you lots of wonderful presents, cross my heart and forgive you everything'. Hermes is delighted. He gives Apollo his lyre and tells him how to play it, and says: 'Now there's no need for you to be so excessively angry with me'. Apollo gives Hermes his shining whip and makes him keeper of his herds.

Off they go together, back to Olympus, where 'wise Zeus was glad and brought them back together in friendship', officially recognising their settlement agreement.[4]

---

4 This is a suggested interpolation, line 568a, but convincing.

Hesiod and Perses

Hesiod, in the eighth century BC, addressed his epic poem, *Works and Days*,[5] to the brother he believed had got the better of him in an arbitration over their inheritance. He complains bitterly not only about the unfairness of the distribution but Perses's idleness and lack of care of the land. Perses refuses to follow Hesiod's agricultural precepts, which include: 'Not a lot of people know that the 27th of the month is the best day for opening wine' and 'Never pee facing the sun.' Instead he spends his time spying and eavesdropping on other people's disputes in the assembly.

While paying the usual formal respect to the lords who arbitrated, Hesiod regularly gives them the epithet 'gift-eating', hinting that it was bribery which caused them to prefer his feckless brother.

---

5 Loeb *Hesiod: Works and Days* pp12–42.

The Boastful Brothers

By their father's will, three sons were to share a pear tree, a goat and a mill, to be divided among them equally.[6] They quarrelled and agreed to go to arbitration.

The arbitrator asked how they thought the tree should be divided. The eldest son said he should have all the wood that was straight and all that was crooked. The middle son that he should have all that was green and all that was dry. The youngest that he should have the roots, the trunk and the branches. The arbitrator said: 'Let the tree belong to the one who can say which of you has demanded the largest portion.'

The brothers agreed that their father's intention was that the goat should go to the son who was able to pray for its greatest increase in size. The eldest prayed that it would be so big that it could drink the whole sea and still have a half-empty belly. The second prayed that if all the wool in the world were woven into a cord, it would not go round the goat's shin. The third that the goat would be so big that a flying eagle would not be able to see its extremities. The arbitrator awarded the goat to the one who could say which had prayed for the largest increase in size.

The mill was to go to the laziest brother. The first said he had been lying in bed for years and that the

---

6 Loeb *Babrius and Phaedrus* pp593–4.

roof had leaked, so that the drops of water had fallen on his ear and bored straight through his head; he was so lazy that he could not be bothered to turn it. The second said that he was too lazy to eat; even if he sat at a table of delicious food for a month, he could not be bothered to eat any. The third said even if he were standing in water up to his chin, he would die of thirst before bending his head to drink. The arbitrator awarded the mill to the one who could say which of the three of them was the laziest.

'Now', said the arbitrator, 'I cannot say which of your answers is the best on any of the three issues. Therefore I ask you to tell me who you think is the winner.' Because each brother claimed that his answer was the best, the arbitrator sent them away with their dispute unresolved.

Brothers and Sisters

There are opportunities for great subtlety even where the facts are clear and no law is applied. In the Han dynasty (206 BC – AD 219) a youth came before the official to recover possession of a sword. His father had been a wealthy man. His wife had borne him one daughter and his concubine one son, the claimant. When the son was only five, but the daughter already married, the father made a will and died. In it he left everything to the daughter, except for the sword, to be the son's when he reached fifteen. Now the son was of that age and the daughter refused to hand it over.

The official considered the evidence carefully. Ownership of the sword was hardly in dispute. But there was more to it than met the eye. The official detected a careful stratagem. This was what the official decided.

The father had wanted the son to inherit; but he realised that if he left everything to him at the age of five the daughter could not be trusted. She would have had effective control of the estate and custody of the son. She was capable of anything and the son would not be safe. Far better, therefore, to let her think she had inherited. She would look after the property well and feel no threat from the son. Moreover, the old man knew her well – she could be trusted to be so mean that she would not even let the son have his sword. But the son would then be fifteen and, if he was anything like his father, would not leave it at that. He would complain to the official. And the official could be trusted to recognise the cleverness of the father and his true intent.

The daughter had had the full benefit of the estate for ten years and that was more than enough. Now it must all be transferred, with the sword, to the son. Tradition has it that all the people – at that time presumably only males counted – greatly approved of this wise decision.[7]

---

7 *Tai Ping Yu Jian (Vol 639): Feng Su Tong Yi.*

Mothers and Fathers

The normal rule in Athens was that a woman could only bring an action through her *kurios* or next friend, usually her father or husband. She could attend the hearing but not be a party or witness. But the rule did not apply to arbitrations.

Plangon, the mother of two boys, wanted their father Mantias to recognise them as his, so that, now they were growing up, they could take their legitimate place in the community and be accepted as members of their father's club. Mantias did not want to accept paternity, but for political reasons he did not want any trouble. He got Plangon to agree to accept a large sum to settle their dispute amicably by dropping her claim. To make their agreement binding, they would get a consent award from an arbitrator. Plangon agreed that when they went before the arbitrator, and Mantias challenged her to swear an oath that he was the father of the two boys, she would decline. The arbitrator would have no choice but to make an award that they were not.

Mantias arranged the hearing, where he challenged Plangon as agreed. In reply she accepted the oath and swore the boys were his. The arbitrator found in her favour and declared Mantias the father. He had no alternative but to assume the parental responsibilities he had been so keen to avoid.[8]

8 Loeb *Demosthenes* IV 'Against Boeotus' I.

3

GODS, GODDESSES AND HEROES

Though the dispute between Hermes and Apollo could be fitted into the last chapter, the other family disputes of the gods and goddesses of Greece justify separate treatment. In any case, their incestuous relationships make it as impossible as it is unseemly to put them into our own more proper family categories.

The Judgment of Paris

Zeus decided that there were far too many humans causing him trouble and that a good war would get rid of an appropriate number. So he sent his daughter Eris (Strife) to a wedding (what better place for family discord – and she was miffed at not being invited) to foment a quarrel between the goddesses. This she did by tossing into the middle of the party a golden apple, inscribed 'for the most beautiful'. Paris got the job of judging the beauty contest between the three finalists: Hera (Juno), goddess of power and Zeus's wife; Athene (Minerva), goddess of wisdom, born motherless from Zeus's brain; and Aphrodite (Venus), goddess of beauty and of love, and Zeus's aunt in a way, having been created from the foam which appeared when Zeus's father Cronos (Saturn) cut off his father Uranus's genitals and flung them in the sea.

None of the goddesses, confident though they were in their own beauty, wanted to risk a fair contest. Hera offered Paris political power, Athene military glory. But Paris accepted Aphrodite's bribe – the promise of Helen, the most beautiful woman on earth.[1] Not surprisingly, Hera and Athene took the award badly and made everybody suffer the consequences, in particular the Trojan War and all the deaths Zeus intended.

1 Loeb *Ovid I: Heroides* XVII.

Calliope: Muse and Arbitrator

The outrageous behaviour of Hera, Athene and Aphrodite as parties to the arbitration of Paris was repeated by Aphrodite again, this time in a dispute with Persephone (Proserpine). Both goddesses were smitten by the beauty of Adonis and wanted him as their lover. They took their dispute to Zeus.[2] He, with a delicacy hardly justified by his own sexual activities – including with Persephone herself, his daughter no less – disdained to arbitrate such a distasteful matter and passed the submission on to another daughter, the Muse Calliope.

Calliope could well be the patron of all arbitrators, because she is the Muse who grants them the gift of honeyed speech, with which they successfully resolve disputes.[3] Aphrodite and Persephone knew better than to try to bribe her. She showed the grasp of essentials that betokens the good resolver of disputes. Weighing up *all* the relevant facts, she hesitated before making the obvious award, that the goddesses should share all Adonis's time. Instead, while still allowing them equality, she divided the year into three parts, one for Adonis to share the bed of Aphrodite, one to lie with Persephone, and the third for him to lie fallow.

2 Robert Graves *The Greek Myths* 2 vols Harmondsworth Penguin 1955 I 18 i 7.
3 Loeb *Hesiod: Theogony* pp79–93.

Unfortunately, Aphrodite did not act in accordance with the award. Once she got hold of Adonis, she charmed him so that he would not leave her.

Momus: Jester and Arbitrator

Zeus, Poseidon and Athene competed to make the most beautiful object. Zeus made a human, Athene a house and Poseidon a bull. Momus (Envy), the gods' jester, was appointed arbitrator. He hated everything. First he found fault with the bull: its horns should have been under its eyes so that it could see where it butted. The human should have had a window you could open in its chest, to see what it was thinking. As for the house, it should have had wheels, so that its owners could take it with them like a caravan, to clog up the roads whenever they travelled. Momus made no award. The moral, so Babrius[4] tells us, after Aesop, is: Never let Envy resolve your disputes!

Momus did not last long in heaven. He boasted he could find fault even with Aphrodite's beauty. Challenged, he scrutinised her naked form diligently but had at last to admit he could find no blemish. As she swayed away triumphantly, though, he announced that her feet made too much noise. That wisecrack cost him his job as jester to the gods and got him expelled from their company.[5]

4 Loeb *Babrius and Phaedrus* Babrius fable 59. *Temple* fable 124 (and note) has other versions.
5 Loeb *Lucian* VI: *Hermotimos, or Concerning the Sects* p519.

The Shield of Achilles

Paris's problem, when he came to collect his bribe from Aphrodite, was that Helen was already married to Menelaus, the Greek, king of Sparta. Paris the Trojan was also married but his wife had no say in these matters. So Paris carried Helen off, a little too willing, and the Greeks attacked Troy to get her back. The Trojan champion, Hector, was Paris's brother. Achilles slew Hector and Paris slew Achilles, despite his divine armour, including a shield which was a work of art.[6]

One of the wonderful scenes which covered the magic shield depicted a city where there were weddings and parties, and music and dancing in the streets, which attracted all the attention of the women and young people. But the men were having a meeting, to hear a dispute about the payment to be made to buy off retaliation for murder.

The murderer claimed the right to make a payment. The kinsman of the victim refused it. The parties agreed on an arbitrator, who was to be advised by the elders. They took turns to speak and two bars of gold were displayed, to be given to the elder whose opinion was accepted by the arbitrator. And all the while marshals were holding back the crowds who were shouting their encouragement of one side or the

---

6 (Old) Loeb *Homer: Iliad I* XVIII 497–508.

other and would have to decide whether the award was fair. Unfortunately, as so often with early law reports, there is no mention of the result.

The Furies versus Orestes

The leader of the Greek forces in the Trojan War was Agamemnon. While he was away his wife took a lover and, on his return, murdered Agamemnon in his bath. Their son Orestes avenged his father. Aeschylus, writing four centuries after Homer, c. 459 BC, portrays the dispute between Orestes and the Furies, whose job it is to deter matricide.[7] The Furies ask Athene to give judgment. She declines jurisdiction but transfers the action to Athens by appointing instead a tribunal of Athenian citizens. Nevertheless, though playing no part in determining the award, she still presides and retains a vote.

Apollo acts as Orestes's advocate and witness – he had demanded Orestes's act and moreover purged him of the blood-guilt. Both sides state their case. The Furies speak on their own behalf, without benefit of counsel. Athene reminds the members of the tribunal that they are sitting for the first time to hear a murder suit which will lay down precedent for Aeschylus's own time and that of his Athenian audience. Each must now cast his ballot.

7 Loeb *Aeschylus II: Eumenides* 433–753.

Both sides make final speeches. Apollo reminds the tribunal of the terrible oath they have taken. The Furies threaten pestilence if the verdict goes against them. But remember! Athene had no mother, having sprung fully-armed from the head of Zeus. She points out that that frees her from any bias towards the mother-protecting Furies and proves it by casting her vote first, on the side of Orestes. Just as well: the ballots turn out to be otherwise even.

The Arbitrator's Caseload

An allusion in the *Odyssey* will bring a sigh from many a weary arbitrator. Odysseus has yet again been shipwrecked and is stuck up a fig tree. There he waits for the wreckage of his ship to surface, in the hope that he will find something to scramble on to, which will get him safely to a more welcoming shore. He has to be patient. Homer writes:[8]

> At the time when a man gets up to go to dinner, leaving the assembly where he has had to decide many disputes between headstrong people seeking his award; only at that late hour did the timbers surface out of the whirlpool Charybdis.

---

8 Loeb *Homer: Odyssey* XII 439–41.

Shakespeare's Hector

Shakespeare claims the last word on the Trojan War. In *Troilus & Cressida*[9] he describes the meeting of Hector, confident and dignified, with his antagonist Achilles, bragging like a modern heavyweight boxer. But first sly Ulysses (Odysseus) foretells to Hector the fall of Troy.

Ulysses:
Sir, I foretold you then what would ensue.
My prophecy is but half his journey yet;
For yonder walls, that pertly front your town,
Yond towers, whose wanton tops do buss the clouds,
Must kiss their own feet.

Hector:
    I must not believe you.
There they stand yet; and modestly I think
The fall of every Phrygian stone will cost
A drop of Grecian blood. The end crowns all;
And that old common arbitrator, Time,
Will one day end it.

---

9 Act IV scene 5 lines 217–27.

4

WOMEN AND ARBITRATION

Can a Woman Arbitrate?

Roman law held that a woman could not be appointed arbitrator, classifying her with the mentally and physically disabled. This was said to be traditional Scots law:[1] 'Women cannot be arbitrators; and it is forbidden to submit a dispute to a madman or someone who is deaf or dumb.' But that probably never was the law in practice and there seems to be authority for the law recognising the appointment of women as arbitrators.[2]

---

1 'Feminae non possunt judicare in arbitrio; item prohibetur compromitti in furiosum, surdum et mutum', *Regiam Majestatem* Stair Society 1947 Bk II Chapter 4 p106.
2 Andrew McDouall, Lord Brankton *An Institute of the Laws of Scotland in Civil Rights with Observations upon the Agreement or Diversity between them and the Laws of England* 4 vols Edinburgh Kincaid and Donaldson 1751 (Stair Society reprint Edinburgh 1993) 455: 'By the civil law, one could not be arbiter in matters brought before him as a judge, nor women ... but the present custom does not exclude ... women, from being arbiters.' The authority he cites is '2 July 1678, Young', a case reported by Sir James Dalrymple, later Viscount Stair. That case would be of the highest authority for Scots law. There are two cases reported on that day brought by different Youngs. Unfortunately neither contains anything specifically on this point, though one does say generally that arbitrators may accept evidence of the existence of a contract which would not be acceptable in a court.

Sunbeams on a Wall of Crystal

There were certainly many writers who saw through the excuses usually put forward for discrimination. Cornelius von Nettesheim wrote in 1509:[3]

> From what hath been said, appears conspicuously, as if written with *Sunbeams* on a Wall of *Chrystal*, That this Sex are not *incapable* of, nor were in the primitive and more innocent Ages of the World, *debarr'd* from managing the most arduous or difficult affairs, till the *tyranny* of Men usurpt the dispose of all business, and *unjust Laws*, *foolish Customes*, and an *ill mode* of education, *retrencht* their liberties. For now a Woman (as if she were only the *passtime* of Mens idle hours, or a thing made meerly for *trifling* Courtiers to throw away their *non*-sensical Complements on) is from her *Cradle* kept at home; and as incapable of any nobler imployment, suffered only to *knit*, *spin*, or practise the little curiosities of the *Needle*. And when she arrives at riper years, is delivered to the tyranny of a *jealous-pated* Husband, or cloistered up in a Nunnery; all publick *Offices* are denied them; implead, or sue at Law in their own Names, though never so prudent, they must not; no Jurisdiction can they exercise; nor make any *Contract* that is valid without their Husbands license; and several other hard *Impositions* they have laid on them.

3 Henry Cornelius Agrippa *Female Pre-eminence ... done into English by HC* [Henry Care] London 1670 p76, quoted by *Murray* pp241–3.

The following examples show how often the formal law must have been broken and men's custom ignored in many places, from the moment that literature has a chance to bear witness to practice.

Doctors of Laws

That women could be both fine legal scholars and practitioners was recognised in the home of revived Roman law scholarship. Franciscus Accursius the elder, the great glossator of Justinian's *Corpus Juris* in Bologna, had a daughter who taught law there in the middle of the thirteenth century.[4] Johannes Andreae, professor of canon law in the same city, had a daughter, born in 1312, who took his lectures when he was away. When she married a lawyer, she handled some of his practice. Two hundred years later, Bitizia Gozzadini (1500–1546) took the degree of Doctor Utriusque Juris from the University of Bologna and gave public lectures. These learned women in their lectures may have commented on the very laws which barred them from doing so. But women's participation, not in learning and legal practice but in arbitration itself, is on record from more than two thousand years before their time.

---

4 This section relies on *Murray* pp245–7.

Eriphyle the Prototype

The first arbitrator on record, who may well be a historical person about whom a myth arose, is a woman who acted as arbitrator twice, in each case taking impressive bribes.

Eriphyle's story is part of the saga of the Seven Against Thebes, so well known that, by the time Homer mentioned her,[5] he did not need to explain who she was. She may have lived, therefore, more than three thousand years ago. She was the sister of Adrastus, king of Argos, and wife of Amphiaraus, a seer. She intervened in their quarrel about the politics of the time, and when they were coming to blows, knocked up their swords with her distaff. They both held her in respect, so they postponed their quarrel and swore to abide by her award not only in the present but in any future dispute.

Adrastus had two daughters. He gave one in marriage to Polyneices of Thebes and the other to Tydeus of Calydon. Both had been driven by political strife from their homes and were keen to be restored. Adrastus decided to deal with Thebes first and called together his chiefs to accompany him on an expedition of war. All agreed except Amphiaraus, Eriphyle's husband. Being a seer, he foresaw his own

---

5 Loeb *Homer: Odyssey I* XI 326.

death in battle. He refused to go and another great quarrel arose between him and Adrastus.

Now Tydeus saw how he could repay Adrastus for his hospitality. He persuaded Polyneices to join him. First he reminded Polyneices of the oath which Adrastus and Amphiaraus had sworn to submit all their disputes to Eriphyle. Then he ungallantly pointed out that Eriphyle was losing her looks. 'She will do anything to stay beautiful. You have in your family an heirloom which Aphrodite gave to one of your ancestors – a magic necklace[6] which will just do the trick. Offer Eriphyle that and she will decide in our favour – even against her husband Amphiaraus.' Polyneices agreed and handed over the bribe. Eriphyle fell for it.

Off they went to war and Amphiaraus was nearly right. He would have been slain had Zeus not cleft the earth below him, just before the spear hit him. And now he reigns, apparently still alive, among the dead down below.

---

6 In other versions it is a girdle or, most pleasing, the saltire, that lovely ornament in the form of a St Andrew's cross which divides the breasts of women in classical Greek dress.

Eriphyle's Come-uppance

Amphiaraus and Eriphyle had two sons, Alcmaeon and Amphilochus. They quarrelled about the wisdom of returning to Thebes to avenge their father. Like the previous generation, they trustingly submitted their dispute to Eriphyle. They knew nothing of their mother's fondness for bribes.

Polyneices had been killed in battle but not before he had told his son, Thersander, of the way to get a favourable award from Eriphyle. Thersander wanted war so much he was prepared to give Eriphyle yet another family heirloom, a dress which was another wedding gift from Aphrodite. She took it and decided for Amphilochus and again for war.

Alcmaeon accepted her award and reluctantly took command of the expeditionary force. This time the Argives were victorious. In the victory celebrations, Thersander's tongue was loosened and he boasted that he should get the credit. If he hadn't bribed Eriphyle, like his father before him, they would never have invaded Thebes. Alcmaeon overheard, and realised that his mother had sent his father to his death for the sake of a piece of jewellery.

Alcmaeon consulted the oracle, which as usual replied with weasel words: Eriphyle *deserved* to die. It did not give him, her son, permission to kill her. But that is what he did on his return. So the Furies drove him mad.

Moral: It is better for arbitrators not to take bribes; better still to be peacemakers not warmongers; but best of all not to get involved in squabbles within their own family.

The Virtuous Arete

Homer mentions another famous woman arbitrator. She must be at least one generation after Eriphyle.[7] In his wanderings after the victory of the Greeks under Agamemnon in the Trojan War, Odysseus puts in to the island of Phaeacia. There the queen, Arete, was honoured by her husband and children more than any other woman. Moreover, Homer tells us:[8]

> The people think she's divine and shout their greetings to her as she goes through the city. She has plenty of decent commonsense, so that – if she feels like it – she arbitrates their disputes. Yes, those of the men as well!

---

7 Because Tydeus, who first thought of bribing Eriphyle, was the father of Agamemnon.
8 Loeb: *Homer: Odyssey I* VII 69–74.

The Celtic Women

Plutarch tells a story about women acting as arbitrators in ancient Italy.[9] Before the Celts crossed the Alps and settled in Italy, there was terrible strife among them. It was deep-seated and went on for years, until it threatened to culminate in civil war. At the crucial moment, the women put themselves between the two armed sides and got them to agree that they should arbitrate whatever was in dispute.

They arbitrated with such unimpeachable fairness that they were able to restore friendship not only between the larger communities but between different kin groups as well. As a result, the Celtic leaders resolved to submit all their disputes to the arbitration of the women. These included matters of war and peace and differences which arose in their relations with their allies.

The reliability and fairness of the Celtic women was accepted not only by the Celts themselves but also by foreigners. When the Celts formed an alliance with the invading Carthaginian African, Hannibal, against the might of Rome, they included in their treaty of friendship a clause which provided that, if the Celts had any complaint against the Carthaginians, it should be decided by Hannibal's officers at his headquarters in Spain. But, if the Carthaginians had

---

9 Loeb *Plutarch: Moralia* III 246.

any complaint against the Celts, it should be submitted to the arbitration of the Celtic women.

The Women of Gaul

The story of the Celtic women is repeated in the context of later dispute resolution by women in France. Jean-Joseph Raepsaet, writing in 1826,[10] names the Countess of Flanders, the Countess of St Pol, the Dame of Peruwez, the wives of the Chatelains of St Omer and Beauvais, and then in a footnote adds:

> The wisdom and prudence of women was highly regarded by the Gauls and Germans. One knows of their Arminia, their Velleda, their Gauda.
>
> Dom Martin suggests that in 1177 BC the Gauls had a supreme tribunal composed of women, called the *Tribunal des Matrones Gauloises*, which decided on matters of peace and war and on disputes between Gauls and their allies and that this tribunal still existed in the time of Hannibal and that in a treaty that general made for his crossing of the Pyrenees and Alps it was stipulated that complaints by a Gaul against a Carthaginian should be decided by the Senate in Carthage but those of a Carthaginian against

10 *Supplément à l'Analyse Historique et Critique de l'Origine et de Progrès des Droits Civils, Politiques et Réligieux des Belges et Gaules etc* Gand Van der Schelden (3rd vol supplmt 1896, vols 1 and 2 1824) Bk 6 Chapter 5 p171.

a Gaul by the *Tribunal des Matrones Gauloises* (*Histoire des Gaules et Gauloises* Bk 1 p243).

Sophe the Dancer Arbitrator

SOPHE
THEOROBA
THYLLIANA
ARBITRIX
IMBOLIA
RUM

That is all there is left to recall the most intriguing of women arbitrators. We know no more of Sophe than is inscribed – not deeply enough, say those who found it – on a square piece of bone dug up in the Santambrogi vineyard, on the left-hand side of the Via Latina about a mile out of Rome.[11]

Sophe's epithet Theorobathylliana shows that she was a dancer in the troupe of the great pantomime-artist Bathyllus, sometimes known as Theoros,[12] who

---

11 Published and described by de Rossi in the *Bolletino del' Istituto* 1873 p152; *Corpus Inscriptionum Latinarum* VI 10028; *Paulys Realencyclopädie der Classischen Altertumswissenschaft* Supplementband X Stuttgart Druckenmüller 1965 sub 'Sophe'; Mario Bonaria *Mimorum Romanorum Fragmenta* 2 vols Genoa 1956 II pp55 and 172.
12 Or, perhaps, there was another actor called Theoros. *Theoros* is Greek for a spectator and *theoria* for a spectacle and in particular a stage show; the background is described in Alan Cameron *Circus Factions: Blues and Greens at Rome and Byzantium* Oxford Clarendon Press 1976.

was the star of the comic stage towards the end of the reign of Augustus (63 BC – AD 14). His followers and students were called by this name to distinguish them from their competitors, the Pyladians, the team led by Pylades.

When Tiberius succeeded Augustus, he set up new annual games in his memory, but the inauguration ceremony was disturbed by the rivalry between the pantomime-artists. Tacitus tells us that Augustus had put up with their rumbustious and disrespectful performances for the sake of his millionaire friend Maecenas, who was besotted with Bathyllus, Maecenas's former slave[13] and the most famous dancer of the moment. 'Besides', says Tacitus, 'Augustus enjoyed this sort of show himself and thought it made him look democratic to participate in the popular entertainments.'[14]

Whatever can be meant by *'arbitrix imboliarum'*? The *imbolia* were the interludes or entractes performed by the pantomime-artists between the acts of more substantial plays. They were a kind of ballet, the descendants of which can still be seen – looking somewhat self-conscious – in nineteenth-century opera, *Faust* and even *Aida* and *La Traviata*. In some way, Sophe was their arbitrix.

Could it be that Sophe was appointed after the rumpus at the inauguration ceremony, to arbitrate the differences between the rival groups of Bathyllus and Pylades? Or were there perhaps two dancers, Theoros

---

13 According to the scholiast on Aulus Persius Flaccus *Satires* 5 123.
14 Loeb *Tacitus: Annals* I 54 (for AD 14).

and Bathyllus, whose quarrels she was most fitted to determine, being the student of both? Did she succeed in restoring peace?

In one way I wish I could find out more. But in another I would have preferred to have found out nothing of her background and had nothing more than her name to go on. Then I could have conjectured that her epithet was given her for her own attributes. The literal meaning of 'Sophe Theorobathylliana' would then be something like 'Miss Clevershins Overfruitedwiththeory'.

Lucrece

As so often, Shakespeare deserves the last word for the sensitivity of his juxtaposition of women and arbitration. In *The Rape of Lucrece*, one of the few things he wrote directly for publication in print, he knew he could rely on his reader's understanding of the nuances of arbitration, mediation and litigation. Moreover, he could appropriately put a sophisticated understanding of those nuances into the mind of a woman. The tragic Lucretia, wretched after being so cruelly and dismissively treated by the king, Tarquin, her husband's friend, knows that there would be no point in trying to explain that she is the innocent and dignified victim of Tarquin's lust and treachery:

> Out, idle words, servants to shallow fools!
> Unprofitable sounds, weak arbitrators!
> Busy yourselves in skill-contending schools,
> Debate where leisure serves with dull debaters;
> To trembling clients be you mediators.
>   For me, I force not argument a straw,
>   Since that my case is past the help of law.

5

THE SORROWS AND REWARDS OF THE ARBITRATOR

Eriphyle was murdered for her pains and other arbitrators have suffered much. Even an honest arbitrator's role may be a dangerous one.

Aristides the Just

Aristides, though a leading politician in Athens early in the fifth century BC, was so honest that he was given the soubriquet 'the Just'.[1] He was much in demand as an arbitrator. Indeed, his enemies suggested that he was taking too much work away from the courts. When he was sitting as an arbitrator, one of the parties told him that the other had done all kinds of things against Aristides's interests. 'I'm not concerned with that', he replied, 'It's your claim I'm hearing, not mine, so stick to the wrongs he has done to you.'

General envy led to his ostracism and the memorable story of the illiterate man who asked Aristides to help him vote. The process was intended to keep politicians humble.

All citizens were asked to choose the person they thought would serve the country best by going into exile for ten years. Then they were to write his name on a scrap of pot or shell and vote with it. Aristides asked the man what name he wanted him to write. He replied 'Aristides'. Aristides asked him why. 'Oh I've never met the man – know nothing about him – but I'm fed up of hearing him called "the Just".' Without a word Aristides did as he was asked. He lost the vote and went into exile.

1 Loeb *Plutarch: Parallel Lives* II.

The Wolf and the Rams

A hungry wolf had his eye on two rams in a field.[2] As he came close he saw they were quarrelling. Being inquisitive he asked what it was all about. They told him they did not know how to divide their ancestral field and asked him to arbitrate. 'I don't know', said the stupid wolf, 'What do you think?' 'Well', said the rams, 'why don't we settle it this way? You stand in the middle of the field. We will each set off from opposite ends and the one who gets to you first wins all.' So it was agreed. They raced full tilt and arrived at the same time, butting the wolf in the belly, and scampered away, leaving him for dead.

2 Loeb *Babrius and Phaedrus* pp593–4.

The Foolish Polymath

Francis Bacon had everything. On Bacon's sixtieth birthday, Ben Johnson wrote:

> Haile, happie Genius of this antient pile!
> How comes it all things so about thee smile?

Leader of scientific thought, literary figure, philosopher and most of all lawyer-politician, his career had vaulted from Solicitor-General to Attorney-General to Lord Keeper to Lord Chancellor, with even a spell as the regent of James I.[3] He fell from grace when at last the courts got round to punishing him for his manifest corruption, and gave up inflicting terrible penalties on those who had been accusing him of it for years.

Three of the twenty-eight charges of bribery which Bacon faced related to an arbitration. The old grocers' company had ganged up with the apothecaries against an upstart society of grocers. Bacon had agreed to arbitrate their dispute. Evidence showed that he had taken £200 from the old grocers, a gold dish from the apothecaries worth £400–500 and – to keep up proper appearances – £100 from the new lot.

Bacon's defence was at first technical. Nothing had been done in court, so he could not be charged with bribery as a judge. On the merits, he had taken from

---

3 All of this section is drawn from a work of fine scholarship: John T Noonan Jr *Bribes* Berkeley University of California Press 1984.

all sides, which showed they were proper fees. Moreover, he wasn't stupid – he could hardly expect to keep something like this secret. Companies (unlike the individuals from whom he had taken bribes) had to keep strict accounts. He wriggled. The amounts he was charged with grew enormous. His enemies, particularly Chief Justice Edward Coke, who had been waiting for his chance for years, finally won the day.

The House of Lords without dissent found Bacon guilty and sentenced him. They did not want to hang him. By a majority vote they agreed not to strip him of his titles. But they sentenced him to imprisonment in the Tower during the king's pleasure; fined him the huge sum of £40,000; and barred him from public office and from Court.

Bacon should have been a broken man but he still retained the royal favour. He stayed in the Tower, when he finally chose to turn up, for only four days. He concocted a document whereby he notionally paid the fine to his own trustees. That meant he not only paid no fine, he took advantage of it to remove that enormous sum from the grasp of his many creditors. He cunningly drafted his own pardon for the king to sign. It restored everything except the right to hold office. All these concessions came at a price. Buckingham, the favourite who had engineered the royal approval, wanted Bacon's London house.

Bacon put Buckingham off. He wasn't quite ready to give up York House but he still acknowledged he needed his patronage with a merry quip: 'I had rather sojourn in a college in Cambridge than recover a good fortune by any other but yourself.' He offered his country house instead. Buckingham did not stoop to haggling. York House it had to be – and now the country house as well. Only then could Bacon be restored to his full liberty and pension.

He never repaid a penny of his ill-gotten gains. He remained in the king's favour, advising on law reform. James knew that Bacon had bribed Buckingham to get royal approval for his various schemes and was prepared to wink at that, moralising hypocrite that he was. But he and Charles who succeeded him always baulked at a full pardon.

The Talking Jackdaw

Bribery does not always bring an arbitrator to a bad end.[4]

A man accidentally killed his neighbour's pet jackdaw. The owner made a very large claim because it could talk. They went to arbitration. At first the arbitrator was inclined to dismiss the claim as trivial; then, when the jackdaw's unusual qualities were explained, he agreed that the loss was great. Then the neighbour pleaded his case. He had nothing much to say but, under his cloak, with just its hem peeping out, was a fine sheepskin. Recognising this for the bribe it was, the arbitrator quickly resumed his former opinion and dismissed the claim.

---

4 Loeb *Babrius and Phaedrus* pp575–6.

From Arbitrator to King

Not love of gold but lust for power may drive an arbitrator to the heights. Herodotus, writing at the same time as Aeschylus in the fifth century BC, mingles myth with the first real attempt at history. He tells the story of Deioces, who started off as an arbitrator, setting himself up 'to profess and practise justice' better than anyone else. Soon he monopolised the work and not only his own townspeople but those from all over Media would submit their disputes to no one else. Then, when he had all the people in his power, he got them to make him king. He built himself a city, Agbatana, ringed with seven walls and would communicate only through messengers, thereby avoiding dangerous contact with those subjects who considered themselves his equals. He was known for hard but fair awards and ruled for fifty-three years.[5]

---

5 Loeb *Herodotus* I pp96–100.

All for Love

Neither gold nor power can get an arbitrator into as much trouble as love. Lord Kilverstoke is handsome, short of money, and keen to marry Ada, an Anglo-American heiress, for her money as well as her looks. Ada is independent – but not too much: 'the masterfulness in him pleased her. The strongest tie between man and woman is protective, which the suffragettes are trying to abolish.' So, when she decides to buy a great estate and create an experimental school, she needs a man, David Inglestone, to make her decisions for her.

> 'You would be a species of referee ... before whom I could try each case.'
> 'Good heavens, Miss Marshall', he breaks into her speech with a merry laugh, 'Do you want me to become an arbitrator ... wishing to make me the arbitrator of the destinies of about six hundred souls?'

The first reform is to let the cottagers buy their holdings by instalments, lending them the money at 1 per cent interest. But there were more peasants than plots.

> It was over the holdings that David was first called upon to arbitrate.
> 'Now this is your first case of arbitration. What do you suggest?'

The wisdom of David is: thirty years' residence shall be the qualification. Then, from the proceeds of sale and interest on loans, build more cottages for the disappointed, all in their turns.

Then the laundry maids refuse to work with Martha, the fallen woman whom Ada has taken under her wing. David's award:

> 'I'm afraid I'm going to be a failure as an arbitrator. I don't know what to say.'
> 'I thought we had agreed that your word was to pronounce the verdict. Isn't that what an arbitrator is for, to decide irrevocably like a judge?'
> 'Yes, but I told you I wasn't capable of being an arbitrator ... Oh, of course I'd keep Martha.'
> She wondered sometimes, did he hate the role of arbitrator?

Not surprising really; the next riddle was worthy of Turandot. Should she give the peasants (that's her name for them) their usual Christmas dinner all together in the barn, or make each an allowance for a meal at home?

It all turns out for the best, of course, but not until there have been the usual misunderstandings when Ada sees David escorting poor Martha home.

> 'Mr Inglestone, you are an arbitrator. I wish you would arbitrate for me. I am in awful trouble and I have so wanted someone to advise me.'
> He looked round quickly. She didn't look as if she were in awful trouble.
> 'The other man doesn't care for me.'

'Are you quite certain?'
'This beats the socialist problem, doesn't it?'
'Oh yes, it beats everything!'
'Yet you are an arbitrator.'
'Not on questions of the heart.'

Selflessly and not knowing of her love for him, David counsels Ada to marry Lord Kilverstoke. But later:

'I didn't do as you said; I didn't listen to your arbitration. I'm not going to marry Lord Kilverstoke.'
'I told you I should be a failure as an arbitrator. You've proved it ... Yes, now I know. You must not marry Lord Kilverstoke!'
'Ah, my arbitrator, my love!'
Their lips meet there before the fire in one long kiss ... For ever now he is at the beck and call of a woman's caprice.

What a lesson for those who take on ad hoc arbitrations with unlimited jurisdiction![6]

---

[6] Lucas Cleeve *The Arbitrator* London Digby, Long & Co 1909. The author in real life was Mrs Georgiana Kingscote, with more than sixty romances to her pen-name.

6

UNHAPPY PARTIES

In fable and story, the parties to arbitration rarely get what they are asking for but often what they deserve, like the wretched Eriphyle.

The Cock who Tried to Bribe the Hawk

Two cocks were in dispute.[1] One of them asked a hawk to arbitrate, expecting that it would kill his rival and eat it. Once the hearing began, however, the hawk attacked the first cock. 'Not me', he cried, 'the other one running away.' 'Oh no', replied the hawk, 'You are the one who should suffer what you wanted to inflict on another.'

The Unwilling Expert

Even if a bird does not instigate the proceedings, her participation may bring her to grief. The poor cuckoo, who is fated never to have a nest of her own, suffered through getting involved in an arbitration to which she was not even a party.[2]

The eagle, ruler of the birds, called them to an assembly. A beautiful empty nest had been found, woven with roses and other sweet-smelling flowers, and many birds were claiming it. He asked the cuckoo to advise the assembly on who should have it. Which bird was the noblest? he asked. The cuckoo could only

---

1 Loeb *Babrius and Phaedrus* p524.
2 Loeb *Babrius and Phaedrus* p524.

say 'Cuc-koo'. And which the fastest? 'Cuc-koo'. Which the best singer? Again the poor cuckoo replied 'Cuc-koo'.

'You shall not be awarded this nest', said the eagle, 'and for your arrogance I declare that you shall never have any other of your own.'

Squabbling Boxers

In 1900, during the Boxer uprising in China, some enthusiasts believed that they were possessed of the god Guangong. When the leader of one group found that two of his men were causing discord by both pretending to be the god, he persuaded them to submit their dispute to him. He then pronounced his award: 'I am the one possessed of the spirit of Guangong. You two are both charlatans and deserve to be put to death.' At the sight of his brandished sword, the disputants both withdrew their claims.[3]

---

3 Paul A Cohen *History in Three Keys: The Boxers as Event, Experience and Myth* New York Columbia University Press 1997 p112, quoting Liu Mengyang *Tianjin Quanfei* p19.

Ingratitude: The Snakes

The ingratitude of parties to arbitration, who refuse to abide by an award when their chosen arbitrator finds against them, can have disastrous consequences.[4]

A soldier found two snakes fighting. The weaker promised to reward him handsomely according to its nature, if he would rescue it. The soldier dismounted and drove off the stronger snake. The rescued snake, recovering its strength, then wound itself round the soldier's neck and started to squeeze. The soldier remonstrated but the snake answered: 'I am giving you the reward I promised. According to my nature, I shall return evil for good, that is the way of the world.'

The soldier protested that he was not getting what the snake had promised at all. They agreed to put their dispute before the next three beasts they met, whose award should be final. The first was a horse. It was in a poor state, thrown out to fend for itself after a lifetime of service to the king. It agreed with the snake that the way of the world is to requite good with evil.

Next came an ox, who agreed with the horse. After a lifetime of service under the yoke, dragging and carrying for the farmer, it expected to be rewarded by being slaughtered for its flesh.

---

[4] In La Fontaine, quoted in Loeb *Babrius and Phaedrus* p560, based on a Persian source, and compare the Chinese story of the Ungrateful Wolf.

But then came a fox: 'Where were you, snake, when you first spoke to the soldier?' 'On the ground, of course.' 'And you, soldier?' 'On my horse.' 'I can't make any decision between you until you both get back to your original position.' They followed the fox's instructions. 'Now then, this is my award: Soldier, go where you please. Snake, crawl on your belly, eat earth and live in a hole – and die miserably as is *your* nature.'

In another version of this fable,[5] the point is the soldier's ingratitude. He promised the fox a bag of cheese for an award in his favour. The fox agreed to the bribe and made such an award. But the soldier substituted a bag with a dog in it. When the fox opened it, out jumped the dog and bit it. Thus the earlier awards of the horse and ox were vindicated.

Ingratitude: The Dragon

A similar Greek fable tells of a peasant and a dragon.[6]

The dragon was beached and gasping by the river. It asked the peasant to lash it on his donkey's back and take it to the dragon's home, promising him great wealth in return. When they arrived, the peasant untied the dragon and asked for his reward. 'You dared to tie me up, a dragon,

---

5 Loeb *Babrius and Phaedrus* p560.
6 Loeb *Babrius and Phaedrus* pp560–1.

and now you ask for gold?' 'That is what you promised.' 'I'll eat you up for insolence!'

They agreed to put their dispute to the fox. The fox tipped the wink to the dragon that it would come down on its side. The dragon smiled. Said the fox to the peasant: 'You fool! How did you come to tie up a dragon? Come on, show me!' The dragon happily allowed the peasant to tie it up as he had found it. Said the fox to the dragon: 'Did he really tie you up as tight as that?' 'Oh, much tighter', said the dragon. 'Tighter still, then', said the fox to the peasant. 'Now, this is my award. Peasant, take the dragon back where you found it and leave it there tied up. That way you won't get eaten.'

Ingratitude: The Wolf

The Greek fables have their Chinese counterpart in a story attributed to Ma Chung-hsi.[7]

A philosopher was stumbling his way through a valley with his lame mule laden with books, when he came across a wolf who had been wounded by a famous hunter. The wolf asked for help, reminding the philosopher not only that he was committed to

---

7 Raymond Van Over ed *Smearing the Ghost's Face with Ink: A Chinese Anthology* London Picador 1982 pp109–15. Though no citation is given, nor any indication of the date this was written, any influence was presumably from West to East.

universal love but also of the rewards that always follow such kindness in fables.

The philosopher put no store by the promise of reward but grumpily acceded to the call on his charity. The sounds of the hunt drew near. To help the philosopher fit him in his bag, the wolf agreed to be bound up in a tight ball. The philosopher took the books out of his bag, stuffed the wolf into it and piled the books back on top. The hunter appeared and demanded from the philosopher any information he had of the wolf's whereabouts. The philosopher practised his craft, spinning out meaningless arguments about truth until the maddened hunter rode off with a headache.

Then the wolf asked to be freed. No sooner had the philosopher done this than the wolf announced that as he was hungry, and the philosopher must abide by his principles, that he should give his life to save others. The philosopher ran round behind his mule and, as the wolf attacked, took care to keep the mule between them.

To end the stalemate, the philosopher suggested that they should put their dispute to three elders in turn: 'If all three agree, then you may devour me. If any accepts my argument, you must desist.' The wolf agreed.

First they put their arguments to an ancient tree. It replied:

'I am an apricot, twenty years old. I was no more than a kernel when the farmer planted me and I have given him and his family sustenance and they have sold the kernels as well. Now I fruit less the farmer has begun to saw off my branches and soon he will fell and sell me. Why should the wolf be more grateful to you than the farmer is to me. Let him eat you.'

The wolf solemnly accepted the award and leapt on the scholar. 'Hold on', he insisted. 'Our agreement was for three arbitrators.' So they put the question to an old ox. He gave his award.

> 'When I was a tiny calf, the farmer bought me for the price of a knife. For years I have worked hard. I pulled not only his plough but the cart. I ate the weeds in his field. It is my labour that has filled his barns and paid his taxes. When I started he was a poor peasant. Now he drinks wine, wears fine clothes and behaves like a gentleman. But I have grown weak and scrawny and he feeds me badly. Even worse, his wife is on at him to finish me off. They are utterly ungrateful. Why, philosopher, should you expect anything different from the wolf?'

In triumph the wolf attacked the scholar again; but he kept his distance behind the mule and shouted: 'Look, there's an old man coming down the road. I have a right to one more arbitration.' The scholar told his tale again, of his own good deed out of entirely unselfish motives and the wolf's ingratitude. The old man sighed and thought deeply. Then he gave his preliminary opinion.

> 'The wolf is in the wrong. To receive a favour and not be grateful brings misfortune. Confucius said that if you never forget a favour you will become as famous as a filial son. This maxim applies not only to humans but to

wolves. You, wolf, seem not to know this. You are probably not a filial son, either.'

The wolf defended his conduct. The philosopher, for all his talk of principle, had not done a good deed out of altruism. He had stuffed all his books back in the bag on top of him. His intention was to suffocate him and sell him. The wolf looked hungrily at both the scholar and the old man.

The old man declared that he was not convinced by either side. He needed better evidence. He would judge for himself whether the wolf was telling the truth when he said he was uncomfortable in the bag. So the wolf allowed himself to be trussed up again and stuffed in the bag. At once the old man asked the philosopher for a knife and plunged it over and over again into the bag. Then he gave his award:

'Philosopher, you are a fool. It is not relevant to the argument that the wolf is hurt by the knife. You meant to be kindhearted but you should not have hesitated to kill such a notoriously savage beast. It cannot feel gratitude. It never helps to jump into a well to save someone who has fallen in. There is no point in taking off your own clothes to wrap them round a freezing waif. There is no merit in choosing your own certain death. Take good note! When charity becomes stupidity, the wise no longer count it a virtue.'

The False Award

A weaver was carrying a bale of cloth to market. When it started to rain, he unrolled the cloth and sheltered under it. A man ran up and asked for shelter. The weaver let him cower under the cloth alongside him. When they got to market, the interloper claimed the cloth was his.

The local official was asked to arbitrate. He declared that the matter was really too trivial for his attention but he would let them know later. Then he sent a servant with his award. The cloth should be arbitrarily divided in half between them. But secretly he had instructed the messenger to note their reaction. The false claimant expressed his profuse thanks to the arbitrator; the weaver denounced his injustice.

When he learned this from the messenger, the official was sure he knew who the true owner was and gave the weaver all the cloth.[8]

---

8 *Zhe Yu Gui Jian.*

Arbitration in Utopia

In fable, at least, a wise and good arbitrator can bring peace and love to all.[9]

A lion became lord of the beasts. He was mild and sensitive and preferred persuasion to force. Aesop says he was 'gentle and just, as humans can sometimes be'. He made sure that there was a regular assembly of the animals where they could resolve all their differences. All the animals could be called to account for what they had done, the wolf by the lamb, the leopard by the wild goat, the tiger by the deer. In this way everybody was able to live happy lives, without fear and at peace with one another. Then up spoke the timid hare: 'This is the day for which I have always prayed, when the weak strike fear into the strong.'

---

9 Loeb *Babrius and Phaedrus* Babrius fable 102; *Temple* fable 195.

The Unwanted Mediator

But the arbitrator or mediator must first have the power to enforce the award. Another fable points a quite different moral.[10]

The dolphins had a long-running dispute with the whales. Up came a crab and offered to mediate. What a joke! As if a nobody in the community could make peace between contending political gangs!

An alternative version,[11] substituting a little gudgeon for the crab, has a more pointed punchline from a dismissive dolphin: 'It is less humiliating for us to fight and die in the attempt than to submit to the authority of a mediator like you.'

---

10 Loeb *Babrius and Phaedrus* Babrius fable 39.
11 *Temple* fable 95.

Arbitration, Faster and Cheaper?

The rare voice of a party to arbitration is heard in John Evelyn's diary for 26 May 1671:

> Having brought an action against one Cocke, for money which he had received for me, it had been referred to arbitration by that excellent good man, the Chief-Justice Hales,[12] but, this not succeeding, I went to advise with that famous lawyer, Mr Jones,[13] of Gray's Inn, and, 27th May, had a trial before Lord Chief-Justice Hales; and, after the lawyers had wrangled sufficiently, it was referred to a new arbitration. This was the very first suit at law that I ever had with any creature, and oh, that it might be the last!

12 Sir Matthew Hale CJ of the King's Bench. Despite his reputation then and now as a wise and learned lawyer and a good, kind and modest man, as late as 1662 he ruled that witches did exist, as a matter of law. As a result, two poor old women were convicted and killed.
13 Not Sir Thomas Jones, later judge of the King's Bench and then Chief Justice of the Common Pleas, because he was of Lincoln's Inn. Quite probably Sir William Jones (1631–1682), later Solicitor-General and Attorney-General, Dryden's 'bull-faced Jonas' whom Evelyn would have favoured as a fellow anti-Catholic activist.

Arbitration Explained

The arguments against arbitration presented by the Taoist philosopher Chuang Tzu are not quite so cogent or as easy to follow:[14]

> Suppose you and I argue. If you beat me instead of my beating you, are you really right and am I really wrong? If I beat you instead of your beating me, am I really right and are you really wrong? Or are we both partly right and partly wrong? Since between us neither you nor I know which is right, others are naturally in the dark. Whom shall we ask to arbitrate? If we ask someone who agrees with you, since he has already agreed with you, how can he arbitrate? If we ask someone who agrees with me, since he has already agreed with me, how can he arbitrate? If we ask someone who disagrees with both you and me to arbitrate, since he has already disagreed with you and me, how can he arbitrate? If we ask someone who agrees with both you and me to arbitrate, since he has already agreed with you and me, how can he arbitrate? Thus among you, me, and others, none knows which is right. Shall we wait for still others?

---

14 Translated in Chan Wing-Tsit *A Source Book in Chinese Philosophy* New Jersey Princeton University Press 1963 pp189-90.

The Arbitrator's Oyster

A far more convincing warning is given by a fable which is worth quoting in full and in its original type:[15]

FAB. CCCCXI

Two **Travellers** find an **Oyster**

As Two Men were Walking by the Sea-Side, at a Low-water, they saw an *Oyster*, and they both Pointed at it together: The One Stoops to take it up; the other gives him a Push, and tells him, 'tis not yet Decided whether it shall be Yours or Mine. In the *Interim*, while they were Disputing their Title to't, comes a Passenger that way, and to him they referr'd the Matter by Consent, which of the Two had the Better Right to the *Oyster*. The Arbitrator very Gravely takes out his Knife, and Opens it; the Plaintiff and Defendant at the same time Gaping at the Man, to see what would come on't. He Loosens the Fish, Gulps it down, and so soon as ever the Morsel was gone the Way of all Flesh, Wipes his Mouth, and Pronounces Judgment. *My Masters,* (says he, with the Voice of Authority,) *The Court has Order'd each of ye a Shell, without Costs; and so pray go Home again, and Live Peaceably among your Neighbours.*

---

[15] Sir Roger L'Estrange *The Fables of Aesop and Other Eminent Mythologies* London 1692.

THE MORAL

Referrees and Arbitrators seldom forget Themselves

REFLEXION.

The Scope of this Fable, is to divert People from Contentious, Expensive and Vain Law Suits. *Agree, Agree,* (says the Old Saw), *the Law is Costly*: The whole Bus'ness of the World is about *Meum & Tuum*; either by Right, in Good Earnest, or by Wrong, under the colour of Right: And while the Clients are Contending about the Title, the Council runs away with the Estate. This Litigious Humour, where Men are as well Stubborn and Wilful, as Captious and Quarrelsome, burns like the Fire of Hell; for 'tis never to be Quench'd: Beside, that whoever is given to Wrangling, can never want Matter or Occasion for't. And this is not only the Case in Matters of Propriety, and in Legal Claims before a Bench of Justice, but it works in a Thousand Instances of Vain Disputations, Competitions, and other Tryals of Mastery and Skill, where there's little more then Pride, Stomach, Will and Vanity, to uphold the Contest. Nay, and he that has the better on't at last, is only the more Fortunate Fool of the Two. Let but any Man set before him the Vexatious Delays, Quirks and Expences of most of our *Barretry Suits at Law*, and 'tis odds he finds at the Foot of the Account, *the Play not worth the Candle.*

7

LANGUAGE TRAPS

One of the reasons why parties may prefer arbitration to litigation is that they can choose their own language rather than that of the courts. This had particular point when the English courts used Law French and kept their records in Latin.

Arbitration and Arbitrage

English now has only one word for arbitration, though it used to have 'arbitrament' as well. German has *schiedsgericht*; French and Dutch have *arbitrage*; Italian *arbitraggio*; Spanish *arbitraje*; Portuguese *arbitragem*. So far so good. But English and German have 'arbitrage' as well, meaning something quite different: trading in documents representing money to take advantage of different prices in different markets. In French and Italian, *arbitrage* and *arbitraggio* are ambiguous, having to do service for both 'arbitration' and 'arbitrage' in English. So if you buy an old code of arbitrage from a secondhand bookseller, you will get a list of those made-up words which penny-pinching senders of telegrams used to employ when buying and selling bills of exchange.

Un Arbitrista

Always interested in anything about female arbitrators, I was delighted to find in a secondhand bookseller's bundle on Roman law an offprint of an article about '*un arbitrista*' of the fourth century AD and the decline of the Roman Empire. I thought the gender of the definite article was discouraging and the text seemed not to be about arbitration at all. Not surprising, because *arbitrista* in Spanish means a schemer or armchair politician.

Arbitrium

Arbitrium in Latin is a trap. Its first meaning was the process of arbitration or the resulting award. It was extended to judgment in the general sense, though not until much later to include the decision of a court. It also came to mean choice – the exercise of will. Working far away from the original sources, in an article on arbitration I came across a footnote reference to a sixteenth-century play, *Libero Arbitrio*, by Francisco Negri Bassanese. As soon as I could get to the British Library I got it out. As I read, it became all too clear that this was a leaden religious debate dressed up as drama, as I should have guessed, even though it was only later that I came across an English translation: *A Certayne Tragedie Wrytten Fyrst in Italian by FNB entitled, Frewyl.*

Gaius Petronius Arbiter

The unprepared literature searcher may feed 'arbiter' into the computer, knowing that Latin and English in some periods as often used 'arbiter' as 'arbitrator', and sometimes drew a distinction between them. The result may then be a plethora of references to that amusing Latin writer, Gaius Petronius Arbiter, whose only connection with the matter in hand is his cognomen, earned as Nero's arbiter of elegance or rather the crony who tried to paint a varnish of style over the emperor's ugly vices. Perhaps he could be the patron saint of spin doctors.

'O Laud'

As if that were not bad enough, from the Middle Ages onwards the Latin word for an award is often *laudum*, with which *laus* (praise) can too easily and comically be confused.

Whatever is a *Brabeion*?

Bound with other *facetiae* in the Bodleian Library is a copy of *Jocus Severus, hoc est, Tribunal Aequum, quo Noctua Regina Avium, Phoenice Arbitro, post Varios Disceptationes et Querelas Volucrum eam Infestantium Pronunciatur et ob Sapientem Singularem, Palladi Sacrata, Agnoscitur.*[1] The author, Michael Maier Com Pal MD, famous alchemist and rosicrucian, says he wrote it on his way from England to Bohemia in September 1616, the year of Shakespeare's death. The title may be translated as: 'The Serious Joke: i.e. the Fair Tribunal by which, with the Phoenix as Arbitrator, the Little Owl is acknowledged Queen of the Birds and sacred to Athene, after various arguments and complaints of the birds bothering her and as a result of her special wisdom.' It is dedicated to all those who love 'true chemistry'.[2]

The whole piece is an allegory. It is not the Owl whose reputation is on trial but Chemistry, 'the art of arts and science of sciences, which all sorts of people every day find fault with, treat with contempt and defame with insults'.[3] Various charges are brought

---

1 Published by Theodore de Brij and printed by Nicolas Hoffmann in Frankfurt am Main 1617.
2 p10: '*Omnibus Verae Chymiae amantibus ... dedico*'.
3 p4: '*Est autem* Noctua *non noctua, sed (de mundanis loquendo) ars artium et scientia scientarum, CHEMIA, quae a diverso hominum genere quotidie accusatur, contumeliis afficitur et convitiis proscinditur.*'

against Chemistry by different birds, which have their own allegorical significance. Just as the Owl is wise, being Athene's pet, the jackdaw is a notorious thief. The jackdaw alleges that Chemistry is no different from a thief, because it steals all your funds, your labours and your years and gives you nothing back but ashes, sadness and gnashing of teeth. The defence addresses the arbitrator, the Phoenix (p55):

Optime Phoenix,	Best of all, Phoenix,
Arbiter aequi,	Arbitrator of fairness,
Pacis amator,	Lover of peace,
Litis et osor,	And hater of lawsuits,
Non ego rixas	I don't intend
Nitor inanes	To bring empty quarrels
Tendere contra	Against Little Owl
Noctuam, ut hostem	As if she were an enemy

The Phoenix makes her award in favour of the Owl. The jackdaw backs off, blushing with shame – presumably a joke. The award is a model of compression:[4]

> Therefore; for pre-eminence in virtue, hard work and intelligence,

---

[4] p75: '*Iudicis sententia ultima:*
Inde mihi Regina avium virtute, labore,
Ingenio, mentis, multiplice doteque praestans
Illa salutanda ac totum est dicenda per Orbem:
Nec quisquam invideat titulos et nomen honoris
Magnifici post hoc vel scripti grande Brabeion.
Sic etenim est conclusum: HAEC STAT SENTENTIA MENTIS.'

Knowledge, and manifold gifts, *Noctua* must be saluted.
Let this now be proclaimed throughout all the world, and let no-one
Afterwards grudge her the name and title of honour: Magnificent,
After this lofty *brabeion*.[5] For this is the solemn conclusion;
    THIS STANDS AS MY AWARD!

---

5 '*Brabeion*' is a poetic Greek word for arbitration, a *hapax legomenon* apparently not found elsewhere in Latin. In Greek it is used by Pindar for the umpire's decision in an athletic contest.

8

UMPIRES

Umpires Nonpareil

Like arbitrators, umpires are private adjudicators. Somehow they break a deadlock, originally by making the number of adjudicators unequal. The word is derived not from 'im-par' but 'non-par', or rather from 'noumpere', by the same process by which 'an adder' came from 'a nadder' and 'an apron' from 'a napron'. It is pleasing that the first citation in the *Oxford English Dictionary*, from an *Aesop's Fables* of 1400, tells of umpires among whom there was neither war nor strife: 'Among these Owmperis was werre none, ne stryf.' There are references there, too, from the fifteenth century, to the rules of guilds, providing that umpires should be appointed if the four arbitrators divided equally in a dispute concerning members.

Not to be Chosen by Lot

The parties to an arbitration often used to provide that there should be two arbitrators, one appointed by each side and that, if they could not agree on their award, they should appoint an umpire to decide. The courts created much learning, some of it respectable, on the appointment of the umpire. The arbitrators must make a conscious and unanimous choice, they said, and not throw dice or draw lots or 'play crosses and bones' to decide between their candidates. But, by a nice distinction, they held that they could draw one name out of a hat, if the parties had agreed that either of the potential umpires whose names were put in would be fit and acceptable.[1]

---

1 *Re Cassell* (1829) 9 B & C 624; *European and American SS Co* v. *Crosskey* (1860) 8 CB (NS) 397.

Welcome Umpires

Almost as soon as there is something which can be called English literature, William Langland's *Piers Plowman* relied on the readers' familiarity with umpires:

> There were chapmen ychose this chaffare to preyse
> That ho-so hadde the hood sholde nat haue þe cloke
> And that the bettere thyng, be arbitreres ...
>
> They couthe nat by here consience acorden for treuthe
> Til Robyn þe roper aryse they bisouhte
> And nempned hym for a noumper.[2]

> There were merchants chosen to appraise these wares
> So that whoever had the hood would not have the cloak
> And that the matter would be better heard by arbitrators ...
>
> But they could not come by their own insight to an agreement on the truth
> Till they asked Robyn the ropemaker to stand up
> And named him as umpire.

It would be interesting to discover when arbitrators in England gave up the practice, which stayed common elsewhere, of ensuring that their award would serve its primary purpose, the restoration of peace between the parties, by giving something (if only a token) to the losing side – so that one party would not get both the cloak and the hood.

---

2 William Langland *Piers Plowman* C VI 382.

Unwanted Umpires

The Merry Wives of Windsor opens with Justice Shallow complaining of Falstaff's affront to him, which he insists was a riot and worthy of the attention of the Court of Star Chamber. Sir Hugh Evans, stage Welshman, tries to calm him down and offers his service as mediator: 'I am of the Church and will be glad to do my benevolence, to make atonements and compremises between you.' And, when Page and Falstaff appear, Evans says: 'Peace, I pray you. Now let us understand. There is three umpires in this matter.' Page: 'We three to hear it and end it between them.' Luckily for us all, no settlement of their quarrel, arbitrated or otherwise, spoils the fun to come, at the expense of the men at the hands of the women.

Milton's Umpire

Cricket, the greatest manifestation of performance art, cannot be conducted without umpires, as Charles Dickens pointed out in *Pickwick Papers*. And no one has been able to encapsulate the bowler's feelings about umpires with the poetic economy of that first and greatest of cricket writers, John Milton. He says it all:[3]

>   Chaos umpire stands[4]
> And by decision more embroils the fray
> By which he reigns.

---

3 John Milton *Paradise Lost* II 1 962.
4 The more usual reading 'sits' is obviously a slip of the pen of a hapless non-cricketing scribe. It is inconceivable that Milton would have written such lines about tennis.

9

ARBITRATION ON THE STAGE

In Menander's Handbag

'A *handbag?*' is perhaps the most quoted line from any comedy; and the most over-used twist of plot may be that which depends on the identification of a foundling by its trappings. But it was still fresh when Menander[1] told the story of Pamphile, raped in the dark at a festival by a drunken youth, Charisius, who later marries her, neither of them realising that they have had a previous encounter. Five months later she secretly gives birth and has the child abandoned in the countryside, where it is found by a shepherd. When his friend, a charcoal burner, hears of this, he asks for the baby to help console his wife, who has just lost hers. The shepherd agrees but is less happy to

---

1 Loeb *Menander* new edn 3 vols 1979 I pp379–526. Menander's comedy *Epitrepontes*, first performed in Athens c. 300 BC, is usually called in English 'The Arbitrants'. This play was known only from fragments, mostly quotations in other authors, until in 1844 a scholar called Tischendorf visited a monastery on Mt Sinai and found in the library three larger fragments in the binding of a manuscript. Then in 1905 Gustave Lefèbvre made an even more remarkable discovery, of a large part of the text, including all the arbitration scene, in the paper-pulp stopper of a deed-jar in a sixth-century lawyer's office in Aphroditopolis in Egypt. The scene is portrayed in a mosaic in a Mytilene from the fourth century AD, which forms the basis of the picture used a frontispiece to this book. Menander is unlikely to have acted as arbitrator himself, and never became a public arbitrator because he died before reaching his sixtieth year, when all Athenian citizens retired from military service and were eligible for appointment. His father's name is on the public arbitrators' list for 325 BC.

hand over the belongings found with it: a shawl, a ring and a silver cup.

Charisius finds out that his wife has had a child and seeks a strangely non-sexual solace with a clever and principled slave girl who plays the harp. The comedy depends on the scene where the shepherd and the charcoal burner dispute the ownership of the child's belongings. They seek an arbitrator and agree to appoint a passer-by, who just happens to be Pamphile's father. His award is that the belongings are the child's and should go to the charcoal burner.

By the time all the misunderstandings have been sorted out in the happiest of endings, the ring has revealed that Charisius is the father, the shawl shows Pamphile to be the mother, and the cup proves the slave girl is Pamphile's long-lost kidnapped sister.

In Plautus's Handbag

In Plautus's comedy *The Rope*,[2] the argument is set out succinctly in a prefatory poem.[3]

> A fisherman pulls from the sea in his net the proverbial handbag.
> In it he finds the toys of his master's lost little daughter,
> Kidnapped and sold as a slave to a pimp. But now she's been shipwrecked;
> And cast ashore she's been saved, by her father – none other – unknowing.
> At last they find out the truth and he marries her off to her lover.

Two slaves, Gripus and Trachalio, quarrel over the bag which Gripus has fished from the sea. Trachalio has no claim but stubbornly insists that they must share whatever is inside. He says they should find an arbitrator and suggests they choose whoever lives in the nearby cottage. Gripus knows that his own master, Daemones, lives there. He happily consents to the appointment.

Trachalio grumbles about being tricked but agrees to allow the arbitration to continue. Gripus's case is simple. Whoever heard of any law that a fisherman cannot

---

2 Loeb *Plautus* pp287–435.
3 The initial letters of its lines make the title in Latin: *Rudens*.
*R*eti piscator de mari extraxit vidulum,
*U*bi erant erilis filiae crepundia,
*D*ominum ad lenonem quae subrepta venerat.
*E*a in clientelam suipte inprudens patris
*N*aufragio eiecta devenit: cognoscitur
*S*uoque amico Plesidippo iungitur.

keep what he catches? Trachalio responds that Gripus may have possession but he has no legal right to the bag. Trachalio knows whose it is. It belongs to a pimp who has survived the same shipwreck. Trachalio knows, too, that it contains a charm bracelet which will enable the kidnapped girl to find her family.

The girl is called to give evidence. She swears that if the bag is opened she will be able to identify every object in the little rush casket inside. If she fails in any respect, she agrees to forfeit everything.

'What is in there?'
'A charm bracelet.'
'Right; what sort of trinkets are on it?'
'First, a tiny gold sword with an inscription.'
'What does it say?'
'My father's name. And a little two-headed axe with my mother's name on.'
'What's this? Your father's name? *My* name, Daimones! ... and your mother's?'
'Daedalis.'
'My daughter!'

Daemones continues to arbitrate on the ownership of the bag, even though he now has an interest in the outcome. He finally awards the bag and the rest of its contents to the pimp. But, following the best practice of traditional arbitrators, he must give something to all sides. Happiness is secured for all when he takes £200 from the pimp in exchange for the bag and its hoard of gold; and uses one half to redeem his daughter's companion from the pimp and the other as the price (payable to himself) for Gripus's freedom from slavery.

Sophe's Successors

Sophe Theorobathylliana danced in entertainments which were forebears of the French *comédie-vaudeville*. Pieces with arbitration in their title, and to a greater or less degree in their plot, seem to have been influenced by Italian models. The earliest I have found were produced in Paris in 1737 as part of the *Nouveau Théâtre Italien*.

The Bailiff Arbitrator

The first is *The Bailiff Arbitrator*.[4] The two lovers are engaged each to the other's widowed parent, Angélique to old Oronte, his son Valence to her

---

4 *Le Bailli Arbitre*, comédie, représentée pour la première fois par les Comédiens Italiens Ordinaires du Roi le 20 juillet 1737 par Monsieur Romagnesi. A Paris chez Briasson.

Jean-Antoine Romagnesi was not Italian by birth. Author of fifty or so pieces for the stage, he was born in Namur, Belgium in 1690 and died in Fontainebleau on 11 May 1742. There may be an even earlier piece but not of quite the same genre: Philippe Poisson *Le Procureur Arbitre: Comédie en Un Acte et en Vers* in Jean Antoine du Cerceau *L'Enfant Prodigue, pièce Sainte ... suivi du Le Procureur Arbitre* Evreux Widow Malassis 1766. The copy in the British Library announces that it will be performed by the 'pensionnaires du Collège de Vernon' at their prize-giving on 28 August 1766. But it was based, perhaps much rewritten for the occasion, on a comedy probably first performed in 1728, see *Le Théâtre de Mr Poisson, Comédien du Roy* 1736. Poisson (1682–1743) was a famous actor.

mother Mme Argante. How to get Oronte and Mme Argante, locked in a dispute over property, to agree to switch generations? The dispute has been going on for twenty years and has now come to be arbitrated by the bailiff, who appears to be a procrastinating lawyer. He has persuaded Oronte and Mme Argante to sign a blank paper, to accommodate whatever shall be his award – a *blanc seing*, or, as we say in English, carte blanche.

Clever servants are needed. They sow doubt in Oronte's mind. Did he know that Angélique had been mentioned in a Paris newspaper in relation to some scandal? Similar concerns are raised in Mme Argante's mind about Valence.

The parties want their carte blanche back. Too late! The bailiff has already completed and inserted his award. Angélique will marry Valence. Oronte and Mme Argante insist that the *blanc seing* depends on their agreement and they agree on one thing: it should be torn up. 'Not so', says the bailiff. 'You made me your arbitrator. You begged me to find a solution to your quarrel. I have done my duty. My award is made. It is final and unchangeable. It fulfils all your wishes and requirements. As far as your property is concerned, I declare that you have made an appropriate settlement on your legitimate heirs, Angélique and Valence. All is in order. You think that I am doing this for a fee. Nothing could be further from the truth. I am doing what I know to be the best for all of you. Don't imagine that you get better justice in town than in the country – just be happy to accept an award given with all possible justice to everyone.'

Reluctantly Oronte agrees, then Mme Argante. As for the lovers, who have engineered the happy ending, they are disingenuously happy:

Valence: 'I don't know enough about business affairs to go against the award of the bailiff.'
Angélique: 'I'm too scared of a lawsuit to rebel against the law.'

Uncle Arbitrator

Perhaps it is not surprising that the French, in the years after their 1789 Revolution, could find fun even in arbitration. A decade later, two comedies about arbitrators appeared in the same year.

On 26 Pluviôse (St Valentine's Day) 1799, Etienne de Jouy and Charles de Longchamps saw their one-act comedy, *The Arbitrator, or the Consultations of Year 7*, open at the Théâtre du Vaudeville in Paris.[5] The scene is the *salle d'audience* of Armand, a magistrate. Edouard, his son, tries to persuade his lover, Ernestine, that all will be well. Armand, who is also

---

5 *L'Arbitre, ou les Consultations de l'An Sept, Comédie en un Acte, en Prose, Mêlée de Vaudevilles* par les Citoyens De Jouy et Longchamps. Représentée, pour la première fois, sur le Théâtre du Vaudeville le 26 Pluviôse an 7. Prix 1 franc 50 centimes, avec des Airs noté. A Paris chez le Libraire au Théâtre du Vaudeville, rue de Malthe; et à L'Imprimerie, rue des Droits-de-l'Homme.

Victoire-Joseph-Etienne de Jouy was a journalist, soldier, socialite, opera librettist and disciple of Voltaire.

Ernestine's uncle, will consent to their marriage. But Ernestine has doubts, and sings a sad little song about the two kinds of love: one with a scarf over its eyes, the other with a scarf over its mouth.

Armand sent Edouard off for three years, until he is twenty-one. Two of those years have passed and the young lovers cannot see why there should be further delay. When Armand enters, they tell him that they have noticed that all those who come to him to resolve their disputes leave happy. Their importunity forces Armand to reveal that Ernestine is not his brother's real daughter. She was left on his doorstep. So no one can give their consent to her marriage until she too is twenty-one, in another year.

The discussions are disturbed by the magistrate's first customers of the day, an old man Valère and a much younger woman Céliante. Céliante wants the rent she says Valère owes her and produces a document. Armand reads it: 'I, the undersigned, promise to pay Céliante, whose attractions are the only ones which can charm me, 3,000 francs rent so long as she can love me. Valère.' He replies that she hasn't loved him for ten years. She says there are women who say they love but don't. She loves but doesn't say. He says her oath isn't evidence enough. She says the ten years make him statute-barred.

Armand says he can see how to reconcile them. The document is a kind of marriage contract, even though it is a little vague. Neither is married to anyone else. Therefore they are free to marry and must do so. 'Hymen discharges the debt of love.'

Céliante agrees at once – 'My hand to you.' 'Aha!', says Armand, 'Céliante must win both ways!' Her immediate acceptance of the marriage is an unequivocal proof of love. For a woman still young and pretty to agree to share her lot with a man who has lost all his money shows a real attachment. That attachment is all that Céliante needs to show to enforce the contract of rent. So it's either marriage or they go back to the contract and Valère must pay up. He concedes graciously.

The Sea-Lion and the Arbitrator

The next application comes from an Italian inventor who in comic Fritalian complains that the government will not pay him for his plan to make the sea rise to the mountains: '*J'ai trovato le moyen di fare grimper la mer ai sommet di piu hautes montagnes.*' The Minister will not grant him a tenth of one écu. The arbitrator declares that this is a matter somewhat beyond his jurisdiction and sends him off with the words: '*Bref! L'enterprise est à veau-l'eau,*[6] *qui trop embrasse, mal étreint.*' I think that means: 'Enough! Your scheme has gone to the dogs. You have bitten off more than you can chew.'

And the sea-lion? If you knew that '*veau-marin*' was demotic for '*phoque*', a seal, what would you think a '*veau-l'eau*' was when you couldn't find it in any dictionary?

---

6 The usual spelling is 'vau-l'eau', with 'vau' from the same root as 'val', so that the phrase would literally mean something like 'vale of water', another pun on the scheme to raise the sea.

Dujardin and the Doctor

'When will people stop quarrelling?' asks Armand, as the next pair appear, M Dujardin and a doctor.

> *Dujardin*: 'I am bringing before you this doctor, who must give me back my ...'
> *Armand*: 'Oh, what is it this time?'
> *Dujardin*: 'My child, that's what!'
> *Doctor*: 'I can't – she's been dead for eighteen years.'
> *Dujardin*; 'You just give her back!'
> *Doctor*: 'But weren't you secretly married, and didn't you ask me to get her adopted?'
> *Dujardin*: 'Yes, but don't you know her address, at least?'
> *Doctor*: 'When I went back everybody there had died or disappeared.'
> *Armand*: 'Hold it! What was the name of the head of the family?'
> *Doctor*: 'Préval, banker.'
> *Armand*: 'And the child's name?'
> *Doctor*: 'Ernestine.'
> *Armand*: 'Eh, Préval is my brother. Ernestine lives here with me! Hold on – this has a touch of farce, it's too much like a modern play.'

And so all ends happily. Armand sings:

> 'What a lovely moment for a weary arbitrator!
> Just for once I've got it right for everyone at last.
> No one's going to quibble or appeal my judgment later.
> All my clients' quarrels are a memory of the past.'

The Lover Arbitrator

Later that year appeared *The Lover Arbitrator*,[7] in which the arbitrator, Volny a lawyer, is the former lover of one of the parties, Mme Lurcé. She appeals to him: 'Whether by design or chance, my husband says he wants you to act as arbitrator between us in our separation. You will refuse, won't you? He must be up to something – he's been such a rotter.' Volny says he has already had instructions to act from Lurcé. Lurcé finds out about the meeting between his wife and Volny and confronts him, accusing him – though he knows nothing of their former relationship – of allowing her to improperly influence his judgment.

Volny insists he will be fair and do all he can to end their differences:

> 'Neither accused nor arbitrator,
> I'll always be conciliator.
> Although a lawyer by profession
> To reconcile is my obsession.
> And so my business always ends
> With no more clients, just more friends.'

---

7 Alexandre-Joseph-Pierre Ségur *L'Amant Arbitre, Comédie en un Acte et en Vers* par Ségur le jeune, Représentée pour la première fois à Paris par les Artistes de l'Odéon le 13 Thermidor An 7 [1799]; à Paris au Salon Littéraire. The Vicomte Ségur, born in Paris in 1756, died in Baguère 27 July 1805, Maréchal de Camp, wrote comedies, tragedies and a sociological work on women.

And so they lay all the documents before Volny. They discuss where they will live apart, the division of property and the arrangements for the children. He will have the son, she the daughter.

Volny chips in – wouldn't it be better for the children to be together, they are so fond of one another? And so it goes. Volny persuades them that it would be much more convenient not to separate the property or even to live in different houses. Then he asks them to repeat that they have sworn to abide by his award. They do.

He says his award has already been completed and he will read it over to them: 'We promise to stand by the award of Volny and comply with its terms in mutual trust, esteem and love – is that all right?' Lurcé looks at his wife: 'Is that acceptable?' 'Mm – yes.' Volny continues: 'They have resolved in unanimous accord to split up their property and separate.' 'Sign that part!' They sign.

'To continue: Their faults, too long denied, they now agree to wipe from their memory forever.' Lurcé agrees 'with all my heart!' His wife mutters 'We can dispute that later.'

Volny goes on: 'Nevertheless, wanting a separation, they have resolved to make it comfortable for themselves – they will live together, with their children, share their property, with the same domicile, eh?' 'Yes' from both. 'One spirit, one heart, one joint intention?' 'Perfect!' says Lurcé. '*Very* interesting' says his wife. 'Very well, let's continue: She from now on deserves the affection which her love has long been denied.' 'Volny!' warns Mme Lurcé. 'Oh, can you blame him?' cries Lurcé. 'With her husband held bound to her wishes and to follow his duty, with tenderness and faithfulness his desire is bound to her virtues by bonds of pleasure.'

'That's it, good man, you've got it!' says he. 'I feel full of happiness and tenderness for him' says she. Volny has the last word:

> 'Let's drink to these bonds which I have been able to reestablish! You love one another! I had to separate and reunite you to dispel the cloud which hid your sweet future. I deserve no credit – I just did my duty. An honest man who searches his soul will never do anything to spoil the happiness of a married couple.'

Seducing the Arbitrator

This was followed a generation later by *The Arbitrator, or the Seductions*,[8] a much more developed piece in two acts.

Two young cousins are stuck in the country and bored. Caroline is pert and lively, Adrien fed up that he has been despatched from Paris to concentrate on his law studies. The play opens with Adrien explaining the

---

8 *L'Arbitre, ou les Séductions, Comédie-Vaudeville en Deux Actes*, Représentée au Théatre de Madame par les Comédiens Ordinaires de SAR le 7 Mai 1827 par Mssrs Théaulon et Paulin Paris 1827. Théaulon was Marie-Emmanuel-Guillaume-Marguérite Théaulon de Lambert; Paulin was Paul Duport, see L-F Hoffmann in (1961) 61 *Romanic Review* 93–108.

dilemma that their host, their older cousin, Colonel Saint-Alvé, is facing. He has no idea what he is in for, agreeing to undertake the noble function of arbitrator.

'Please', says Caroline, wide-eyed, 'explain arbitration for me.' Adrien unloads his recently acquired learning: 'An arbitrator – article 57 of the Civil Code – is a judge whom the law permits you to choose for yourself and who judges either at first instance or finally, as the parties agree. So the award which my cousin is going to make in the Desormes affair will be final and definitive, according to article 267 of the Code, as both plaintiff and defendant have agreed.' 'Oh, what a lovely law!', says Caroline, 'but what's all the fuss about?'

Adrien explains: 'Desormes is a spiteful old devil. The Comtesse d'Erli is so pretty, everybody adores her, if only I were the arbitrator!' 'And what about justice, then?' asks Caroline. 'Oh, justice ... well, fair enough, but a good-looking woman shouldn't be in the wrong. It seems that about 1786, before the Revolution, Baron Desormes realised that he would have to flee, and made a fake sale of his property to the Comte d'Erli, who made a counter-sale back to the Baron. Now d'Erli's widow and the Baron are in dispute over it.'

The Baron discovers that the Colonel is in love with his adversary. He believes his case is hopeless and offers to settle for a third of the claim. 'No', says the Comtesse, 'You wanted a fight – you've got one!' 'Oh, all right, a half'. 'Don't even think about it!' Later the poor man increases his bid to two-thirds. Still he is rejected.

The matter comes on for hearing before the Colonel. The Baron gets nasty. There's no hope of a fair hearing, he alleges. The Colonel gets on his high horse. 'You doubt my honour, then?' The Baron apologises. The award is read out:

> 'I, Saint-Alve, retired colonel, by virtue of the powers of sovereign arbitration conferred on me by the agreement of both parties, declare that the counter-sale letter, signed by the Comte d'Erli, is good and valid and, according to the powers vested in me by the parties, I declare that the Baron Desormes shall recover all the property which was his father's.'

All: 'Good Heavens!'

The Comtesse asks Adrien: 'Shall I accept the Colonel's proposal of marriage?' The law student replies: 'It is permitted by the Civil Code article ...' The Baron blesses the union: 'I have made you two my heirs but, if you don't mind waiting just a little longer to collect!'

The Colonel declares he will never take on another arbitration, above all when pretty women are involved – it's too dangerous. All sing:

> 'In these scenes of irreverent laughter
> The public is judge of our fate.
> In the theatre there's only one master.
> And you must, dear friends, arbitrate.
>
> It matters far more than a title
> For us who depend on your power.
> We just hope we can always seduce you –
> Until next time we say: "Au revoir!"'

Gaîté Parisienne

Arbitration lives on in the world of French theatre. Manuel Rosenthal, who put together pieces of the works of Offenbach to provide the music for *Gaîté Parisienne* for the Ballets Russes, took his completed score to the choreographer Leonid Massine for approval. Massine heard him play it through and pronounced his rejection, on the ground that it was disrespectful to Offenbach. Rosenthal reports:[9]

> I thought: 'Arguing with him won't get me anywhere – he'll stick to his opinion and I'll stick to mine. That's all; we can't fight.' And I had an extraordinary idea. I said: 'Are you prepared to accept arbitration?' He said: 'Yes, perhaps, but who?' My next thought was one of genius: Stravinsky!

All agreed and convened at Stravinsky's place. Rosenthal played through the score. Then Stravinsky took Massine by the collar: 'Leonid, if you turn this score down, you will probably turn down the biggest hit of your career.' That was that!

---

9 *BBC Music Magazine* December 1999 p138.

Resolution

Perhaps the best story about mediation was told by Alexandre de la Roche, Prior of St Pierre in 1665.[10] An incompetent but likeable mediator had no idea how to bring the parties to a settlement. After every adjournment, he wined and dined with the parties until he became their friend. No nearer a resolution of their dispute, but increasingly unwilling to offend him, they decided to drop it. Or, as John Milton puts it:[11]

> 'What reinforcement we may gain from hope;
> If not, what resolution from despair.'

---

10 For the full story, it will be necessary to read my *The Charitable Arbitrator* (forthcoming from Holo Books), which includes a translation of [Alexandre de la Roche] *Pour Eviter les Procez* Paris Raveneau 2nd edn 1668
11 *Paradise Lost* I 190.

Index

Accursius 52
Achilles 45, 48
Ada 70–2
Adonis 43
Adrastus 53–4
Adrien 119–22
Aeschylus 46, 68
Aesop 83, 97
Africa 57
Agamemnon 46, 56
Agbatana 69
Aida 60
Alcmaeon 55
Alps 57
America 70
Amphiaraus 53–5
Amphilochus 55
Andreae 52
Angélique 108
Anstey 11
Aphrodite 42–5, 54, 55
Apollo 33–5
apothecaries 66
apple 42
apricot 79
arbiter 91–2
arbitrage 90
Arbitrants 2, 103
Arbitrator, or the Consultations of Year VII 110
Arbitrator, or the Seductions 119
arbitrista 91
arbitrium 91
Archidamus II 20
Arete 56
Argante 108
Argos 53
Aristides 64
Armand 110–15
Arminia 58
Athene 20, 42, 44, 94
Athenian 20, 64, 103
Athens 20, 64
audi alteram partem! 19
Augustus 60

baby 103–4
Bacon, Francis 66
Bacon, Matthew 16–17
bailiff 108–9
Bailiff Arbitrator 108–9
barrister 8
Bassanese 91
Bathyllus 59–61
Beauvais 58
bees 26–7

bill of exchange 90
blanc seing 108
Bodleian Library 93
Bohemia 93
Bologna 52
books 78–81
Bowen 10
Boxers 75
brabeion 93–5
bribery 36, 66–8
brothers 30–9
Buckingham 67
bull 44

Calliope 43
Calydon 53
Campbell 10
Cambridge 67
Caroline 119–22
Carthaginian 57–8
cattle 33–5
Céliante 111–12
Celts 57
Certayne Tragedie ... entitled, Frewyl 91
Chang 17–18
Chaos 101
charcoal burner 103
Charisios 103–4
Charitable Arbitrator 123
Charles I 68
Chartered Institute of Arbitrators 6, 9, 13
Charybdis 47
chemistry 93–5
China 17–18, 21–6, 75, 78–81, 86
Chinese 8, 9

Christmas 71
Chuang Tzu 86
Civil Code 119, 122
clan 23, 31
cloak 68
cock 74
Cocke 85
Coke 67
community 23–4
Comyn 16
Common Law 16
Common Pleas 85
concubine 38
Confucian 24–5, 30, 80
Confucius 22, 80
construction 12
cooking 15
Corpus Juris 52
cows 33–5
crab 84
cricket 101
criminal offence 34
cuckoo 74
Cyllene 33

D'Erli 120–2
Daedalis 106
Daemones 106–7
dancing 59–61
daughter 38–9
deer 28–9, 83
defence 34
Deioces 69
De Jouy 110
De la Roche 123
De Longchamps 110
Desormes 120–2

dice 98
Dickens 101
disabilities 16–17, 20–1
doctor 114–15
dog 77
dolphin 84
donkey 77
dragon 77–8
drones 26–7
Dryden 85
ducks 17–18
Dujardin 114–15
Dutch 90

eagle 37, 74
Edouard 110
English 90
Epitrepontes 2, 103
Eriphyle 53–6, 63, 73
Eris 42
Ernestine 110–11, 115
Evans 100
Evelyn 85
expert 20–1, 74–5

Falstaff 100
family 23–40
farmer 17–18
fathers 31–40
Faust 60
fees 88
fig 47
fisherman 105–6
Flanders 58
food 15
fox 77–8
French 90, 107–22

Fritalian 112
Fujian 23–4
Furies 46–7

Gaîté Parisienne 123
Gauda 58
Gaul 58–9
German 90
Germans 58
goat 37, 83
gold 45
Gozzadini 52
Gray's Inn 85
Greece 19–20, 33–6, 40–8,
    53–6, 64, 103–4
Greek 95
Gripus 105–7
grocers 66
Guangong 75
gudgeon 84

Hale 85
Han 38
handbag 103–7
Hannibal 57
hare 83
hawk 74
heaven 44
Hector 48
hedgehog 28–9
Helen 42
hell 88
Hera 42
Hermes 33–5
Herodotus 69
Hesiod 19, 36
history of arbitration 9

Homer 46, 56
Hong Kong 7
horse 20–1, 76–7
house 44
House of Lords 67
hunter 78–81
husband 40
Hymen 111

Iliad 45–6
imbolia 60
infants 17
Inglestone 70–2
Institucion of a Gentleman 18
international arbitrators 12
interpreters 8
Italian 90, 107
Italy 57

jackdaw 68, 94
James I 66
jewellery 104–6
Jiangxi 23
Jocus Severus 93–5
Johnson 66
Jones 85
Juno 42
Jupiter 33–5, 42–4, 47
jurisdiction 46
Justinian 52

Kilverstoke 70–2
kings 66–9
King's Bench 85

lamb 83
land 36

Langland 99
Latin 19, 27, 89, 91–2
laudum 92
Law French 89
lawyers 11, 53
Legalists 22
leopard 73
Lesbos 2
Lincoln's Inn 85
lion 83
Loeb Classical Library 12
lot 98
love 72
Lover Arbitrator 115
Lucretia 62
Lurcé 115–18

Ma Chung-hsi 78
Maecenas 60
magistrate 18–19
Maier 93
Mantias 40
Mao 22
market 82
marriage 42, 103, 107, 109, 112, 115–18, 122
Martha 71
Martin 58
Massine 123
Media 69
Megarry 7
Menander 2, 103
Menelaus 45
mental capacity 16–17
Merry Wives of Windsor 100
Milton 101, 123
Minerva 20, 42, 44, 94

Ming Dynasty 21
Momus 44
mothers 26
mule 78–81
murder 45–6
music 34, 45
Mytilene 2, 103

Nero 92
Nouveau Théâtre Italien 107

Odysseus 47, 48, 56
Odyssey 47, 53, 56
Offenbach 123
official 18, 21–5
Olympus 35
opera 60
Orestes 46–7
Oronte 108
ostracism 64
owl 93–5
ox 76, 80
oyster 87

Page 100
Pamphile 103–4
Paris, France 107
Paris of Troy 42
pear 37
peasants 71, 77–8
Persephone 43
Perses 36
Peruwez 58
Petronius 92
Phaeacia 56
Phaedrus 26–7
philosopher 78–81

phoenix 93–5
Pickwick Papers 101
Piers Plowman 99
pimp 105–7
Pindar 95
Plangon 40
Plautus 105–6
Plutarch 19, 57
Poisson 108
Polyneices 53–5
Pomponius 16
Portuguese 90
Poseidon 44
Pour Eviter les Procez 123
Precepts of Chiron 19
Préval 115
Proserpine 43
Pucheng 23
purse 19
Pylades 60
Pylos 33
Pyrenees 58

Raepsaet 58
ram 65
Rape of Lucrece 62
referees 88
Regiam Majestatem 50
Robyn the ropemaker 99
roebuck 28–9
Romagnesi 108
Roman law 16, 52, 91
Rome 59
Rope 105–7
Rosenthal 123
Rudens 105–7

Saint-Alvé 119–22
Santambrogi 59
scholars 17–18, 78–81
Scots law 50
sea 37
sea-lion 112
Segur 115
Seven Against Thebes 53
Shakespeare 48, 62, 100
   The Merry Wives of Windsor 100
   The Rape of Lucrece 62
   Troilus and Cressida 48
Shallow 100
shepherd 103
shield 45
ship 47
shipwreck 47, 106
slave girl 104
snakes 76–7
socialists 72
soldier 76–7
Sophe 59–61, 107
Spain 57
Spanish 90–1
Sparta 20
spin doctors 92
St Omer 58
St Pol 58
stage 102-2
Star Chamber 100
Stravinsky 123
suffragettes 70
surveyors 12
sword 38–9

Tacitus 60

Taoist 86
Tarquin 62
telegram 90
temple 20
Thebes 53–6
Theorobathylliana 59, 107
Theoros 59, 60
thief 94
Tiberius 60
tiger 83
time 48
The Times 10
torture 31
The Tower 67
Trachalio 105–7
Traviata 60
trees 37, 79
Tribunal des Matrones Gauloises 58–9
Troilus and Cressida 48
Trojans 48, 56
Turandot 71
Tydeus 53

Ulysses 47, 48, 56
umpires 96–101
Uranus 42

Valence 108
Valère 111–12
vaudeville 107–22
Velleda 58
Venus 42–5, 54, 55
Via Latina 59
Volny 115–18

weaver 82

wedding 42
Welsh 100
West 15–19
whale 84
wife 103, 107, 109, 112, 115–18, 122
will 24
wine 36

wolf 65, 78–81, 83
wood 37

Xi Zhou 25

Zeus 33–5, 42–4, 47
Zhou 25
Zhou Wen Wang 25

ABOUT THE AUTHOR

Derek Roebuck, a solicitor and associate member of the Chartered Institute of Arbitrators, is a Senior Associate Research Fellow at the University of London's Institute of Advanced Legal Studies and Guest Professor at the People's University of China, Peking. He has held chairs of law and comparative law in Australia, Papua New Guinea and Hong Kong and has had forty books published on law, legal history and language, including *The Background of the Common Law* (Oxford University Press 2nd edn 1990), and the *Chinese Digest of Hong Kong Law* (Peking University Press 7 vols 1995–97). His most recent publication is with his wife Susanna Hoe *The Taking of Hong Kong* (Curzon 1999). He is now writing a comparative history of arbitration in practice, which has so far produced 'A Short History of Arbitration' in Kaplan, Spruce and Moser *Hong Kong and China Arbitration* (Butterworths 1994) and 'Sources for the History of Arbitration' [1998] 14 *Arbitration International*. He has just completed a volume on arbitration in ancient Greece.

ALSO FROM HOLO BOOKS

The Arbitration Press

A History of Arbitration in Ancient Greece
Derek Roebuck

The development of methods of resolving disputes by mediation and arbitration in the Greek world, over eight centuries from the time of Homer to 30 BC, when the Romans took Alexandria. The first full-length study using (and reproducing in translation) the primary sources, not only the rich literature of epic, drama, history, philosophy and oratory, but also inscriptions and papyri.

The Charitable Arbitrator
Derek Roebuck

A manual of the practice of mediation and arbitration in Louis XIV's France, with a lively and challenging call for law reform, translated with an introduction to the historical and legal background; the characters, including individual arbitrators and patrons; the mystery of the author; and the plates, which depict the practice of arbitration in mid-seventeenth-century France.

ALSO FROM HOLO BOOKS

The Women's History Press

Women at the Siege, Peking 1900
Susanna Hoe

The Boxer uprising; the siege of the legations; 55 days in Peking; foreign troops looting China's capital. These are images from books and films over the past hundred years. Now the story is told from the women's point of view, using their previously neglected writings. This is the author's fourth book about foreign women and China. It adds to the essential body of women's history and gives a truer picture of what happened just a century ago.